WHY READ AND STUDY THE GOSPEL OF JOHN?

Following Jesus isn't just about what happens when you die, or what happens at the end of the world.

The Christian religion isn't just a hollow shell, all form and no substance. Behind it are the most profound and evocative truths that God has revealed in human history. These truths find their ultimate expression in the person of Jesus.

Jesus isn't some vague historical figure you can only guess about. You don't have to wonder what he was like, what he thought and did, or even if he existed at all. Jesus is someone we can know about, and get to know personally, even today.

Who says so? One of the people who was closest to Jesus when he lived on earth, his good friend John. At the end of his life, John wrote down the most important things he remembered and understood about Jesus, so that others could know him as he had. The book he wrote is called the gospel of John.

Get together with some friends and use this guide to go through that book. You'll discover what an exciting, profound, and powerful person Jesus is. You'll find that his message has relevance for your life today. You'll see how his life and words embody the deepest meaning behind the religion you might have thought was only a shell. And you may just meet Jesus personally.

That's what John was hoping for. At the end of his book he explained, "These are written that you may believe that Jesus is the Messiah, the Son of God, and that by believing you may have life in his name." Read the book. Life is waiting for you inside it.

UNDERSTANDING THE
BOOKS OF THE BIBLE

JOHN

Also available in the
UNDERSTANDING THE BOOKS OF THE BIBLE series:

Genesis—July 2010
Wisdom: Proverbs/Ecclesiastes/James—October 2010
Biblical Apocalypse: Daniel/Revelation—October 2010

Future releases:

Exodus/Leviticus/Numbers
New Covenants: Deuteronomy/Hebrews
Joshua/Judges/Ruth
Samuel–Kings

Amos/Hosea/Micah/Isaiah
Zephaniah/Nahum/Habakkuk
Jeremiah/Obadiah/Ezekiel
Haggai/Zechariah/Jonah/Joel/Malachi

Psalms Books 1–3
Psalms Books 4–5/Song of Songs/Lamentations
Job
Chronicles/Ezra/Nehemiah/Esther

Matthew
Mark
Luke–Acts

Thessalonians/Corinthians/Galatians/Romans
Colossians/Ephesians/Philemon/Philippians/Timothy/Titus
Peter/Jude/John

JOHN

Christopher R. Smith

Biblica Publishing
We welcome your questions and comments.

USA   1820 Jet Stream Drive, Colorado Springs, CO 80921
India   Logos Bhavan, Medchal Road, Jeedimetla Village, Secunderabad 500 055, A.P.

UNDERSTANDING THE BOOKS OF THE BIBLE: John
ISBN-13: 978-1-60657-054-8

A catalog record for this book is available through the Library of Congress.

Printed in the United States of America

CONTENTS

HOW THESE STUDY GUIDES ARE DIFFERENT

Did you know you could read and study the Bible without using any chapters or verses? The books of the Bible are real "books," and they're meant to be experienced the same way other books are: as exciting, interesting works that keep you turning pages right to the end and then make you want to go back and savor each part. The UNDERSTANDING THE BOOKS OF THE BIBLE series of study guides will help you do that with the Bible.

While you can use these study guides with any version or translation, they're especially designed to be used with *The Books of The Bible*, an edition of the Scriptures from Biblica that takes out the chapter and verse numbers and presents the biblical books in their natural form. Here's what people are saying about reading the Bible this way:

I love it. I find myself understanding Scripture in a new way, with a fresh lens, and I feel spiritually refreshed as a result. I learn much more through stories being told, and with this new format, I feel the truth of the story come alive for me.

Reading Scripture this way flows beautifully. I don't miss the chapter and verse numbers. I like them gone. They got in the way.

I've been a reader of the Bible all of my life. But after reading just a few pages without chapters and verses, I was amazed at what I'd been missing all these years.

For more information or to download the gospel of John from *The Books of The Bible,* visit http://www.thebooksofthebible.info. Premium editions of this Bible will be available in Spring 2011 from Zondervan at your favorite Christian retailer.

For people who are used to chapters and verses, reading and studying the Bible without them may take a little getting used to. It's like when you get a new cell phone or upgrade the operating system on your computer. You have to unlearn some old ways of doing things and learn some new ones. But it's not too long until you catch on to how the new system works and you find you can do a lot of things you couldn't do before.

Here are some of the ways you and your group will have a better experience of the Scriptures by using these study guides.

YOU'LL FOLLOW THE NATURAL FLOW OF BIBLICAL BOOKS

This guide will take you through the gospel of John following its natural flow. (The way the book unfolds is illustrated on page 8.) You won't go chapter-by-chapter through John, because chapter divisions often come at the wrong places and break up the flow. Did you know that the chapter divisions used in most modern Bibles were added more than a thousand years after the biblical books were written? And that the verse numbers were added more than three centuries after that? If you grew up with the chapter-and-verse system, it may feel like part of the inspired word of God. But it's not. Those little numbers aren't holy, and when you read and study John without them, you'll hear the story emerge as never before.

To help you feel where you are in the book's natural flow, each study session will be headed by a visual cue, like this:

**Gospel of John > Book of Signs >
First Section: Jesus as the New Creation**

YOU'LL UNDERSTAND WHOLE BOOKS

Imagine going to a friend's house to watch a movie you've never seen before. After only a couple of scenes, your friend stops the film and says, "So, tell me what you think of it so far." When you give your best shot at a reply, based on the little you've seen, your friend says, "You know, there's a scene in another movie that always makes me think of this one." He switches to a different movie and before you know it, you're watching a scene from the middle of another film.

Who would ever try to watch a movie this way? Yet many Bible studies take this approach to the Bible. They have you read a few paragraphs from one book of the Bible, then jump to a passage in another book. The UNDERSTANDING THE BOOKS OF THE BIBLE series doesn't do that. Instead, these study guides focus on understanding the message and meaning of one book. This guide will make limited references to other biblical books only when the gospel of John itself alludes to them.

Your group will read through the entire gospel of John, not just selected chapters or verses. Two of the sessions (session 2 and session 14) are overviews that together involve reading through the entire text of John, in preparation for considering individual sections. Reading through all of John's gospel will be like viewing a whole movie before zooming in on one scene.

Groups that read books of the Bible aloud together have a great experience doing this. (If you've never done it before, give it a try—you'll be surprised at how well it flows and how fast the time passes.) You can read the first part of John in one meeting and the second in another meeting, or you can schedule a longer meeting to read both parts, with a break in the middle for refreshments or a meal. For these overview studies, the discussion will be briefer and designed to allow people to share their overall impressions.

YOU'LL DECIDE FOR YOURSELVES
WHAT TO DISCUSS

In each session of this study guide there are many options for discussion. While each session could be completed by a group in about an hour and a half, any one of the questions could lead to an involved conversation. There's no need to cut the conversation short to try to "get through it all." As a group leader, you can read through all the questions ahead of time and decide which one(s) to begin with, and what order to take them up in. If you do get into an involved discussion of one question, you can leave out some of the others, or you can extend the study over more than one meeting if you do want to cover all of them.

TOGETHER, YOU'LL TELL THE STORY

Each session gives creative suggestions for reading the passage you'll be discussing. The guide will often invite the group to dramatize the Scriptures by reading them out loud like a play. The discussion options may also invite group members to retell the biblical story from a fresh perspective. This kind of telling and retelling is a spiritual discipline, similar to Bible memorization, that allows people to personalize the Scriptures and take them to heart. Our culture increasingly appreciates the value and authority of story, so this is a great discipline for us to cultivate.

EVERYBODY WILL PARTICIPATE

There's plenty of opportunity for everyone in the group to participate. Because the gospel of John is a story with characters, as you read from it in each session you'll often have different group members taking the parts of different characters. Group members can also read the session introduction aloud or the discussion questions. As a leader, you can easily involve quiet people by giving them these opportunities. And everyone will feel that they can speak up and answer the questions, because the questions aren't looking for "right answers." Instead, they invite the group to work together to understand the Bible.

YOU'LL ALL SHARE DEEPLY

The discussion questions will invite you to share deeply about your ideas and experiences. The answers to these questions can't be found just by "looking them up." They require reflection on the meaning of the whole passage, in the wider context of the gospel of John, in light of your personal experience. These aren't the kinds of abstract, academic questions that make the discussion feel like a test. Instead, they'll connect the Bible passage to your life in practical, personal, relational ways.

To create a climate of trust where this kind of deep sharing is encouraged, here are a couple of ground rules that your group should agree to at its first meeting:

- *Confidentiality.* Group members agree to keep what is shared in the group strictly confidential. "What's said in the group stays in the group."
- *Respect.* Group members will treat other members with respect at all times, even when disagreeing over ideas.

HOW TO LEAD GROUP STUDIES USING THIS GUIDE

Each session has three basic parts:

Introduction to the Study

Have a member of your group read the introduction to the session out loud to everyone. Then give group members the chance to ask questions about the introduction and offer their own thoughts and examples.

Reading from the Gospel of John

Read the selection out loud together. (The study guide will offer suggestions for various ways you can do this for each session. For example, sometimes you will assign different characters in the story to different readers, and sometimes different people will read different sections of the passage.)

Discussion Questions

Most questions are introduced with some observations. These may give some background to Jewish culture, or explain where you are in the flow of the story. After the observations there are suggested discussion questions.

Many of them have multiple parts that are really just different ways of getting at an issue.

You don't have to discuss the questions in the order they appear in the study guide. You can choose to spend your time exploring just two or three questions and not do the others. Or you can have a shorter discussion of each question so that you do cover all of them. As the group leader, before the meeting you should read the questions and the observations that introduce them, and decide which ones you want to emphasize.

When you get to a given question, have someone read aloud the observations and the question. As you answer the question, interact with the observations (you can agree or disagree with them) and with the reading from the gospel of John. Use only part of the question to get at the issue from one angle, or use all of the parts, as you choose.

Sometimes there will be things to do or think about in preparation for your next session. But there's never any "homework" in the traditional sense. Whenever a session ends with a section called "For Your Next Meeting," have someone read this information aloud to the group to explain how people should prepare for the next study.

TIPS FOR HOME GROUPS, SUNDAY SCHOOL CLASSES, CHURCH-WIDE BIBLE EXPERIENCES, AND INDIVIDUAL USE

If you're using this guide in a *home group*, you may want to begin each meeting (or at least some meetings) by having dinner together. You may also want to have a time of singing and prayer before or after the study.

If you're using this guide in a *Sunday school class*, you may want to have a time of singing and prayer before or after the study.

This study guide can also be used in connection with a *church-wide Bible experience* of the gospel of John. If you're using it in this way:

- Encourage people to read each session's Scripture passage by themselves early in the week (except for sessions 2 and 14, when the whole church will gather to hear the gospel of John read out loud).

- Do each session in midweek small groups.
- Invite people to write/create some response to each small-group session that could be shared in worship that weekend. These might involve poetry, journal or blog entries, artwork, dramas, videos, and so on.
- During the weekend worship services, let people share these responses, and have preaching on the Scripture passage that was studied that week. Preachers can gather up comments they've heard from people and draw on their own reflections to sum up the church's experience of that passage.

This guide can also be used for *individual study*. You can write out your responses to the questions in a notebook or journal. (However, we really encourage reading and studying the Bible in community!)

OUTLINE OF THE GOSPEL OF JOHN

Prologue

THE BOOK OF SIGNS

(Jesus & the New Creation)
Jesus starts in Judea and travels to Galilee
The First Seven Days: Jesus Makes Disciples
Wedding in Cana ●

(Jesus & the Temple)
Jesus goes to Jerusalem for Passover and returns to Galilee
Cleanses the Temple ■
Nicodemus ■
Samaritan Woman
The Royal Official ●

(Jesus & the Sabbath)
Jesus goes to Jerusalem for another festival
Heals a Lame Man ●
Dispute with Pharisees ■

(Jesus & the Exodus)
Jesus in Galilee
Feeds the Crowds ◆
Walks on Water ●
Bread of Life ■ ●

(Jesus & Tabernacles)
Jesus goes to Jerusalem for Festival of Tabernacles
Light of the World ◆ ■
Dispute with Pharisees ■
Heals a Blind Man ◆ ◆ ●
Dispute with Pharisees ■

(Jesus & Dedication)
Jesus goes to Jerusalem for Dedication Festival
Jesus is one with the Father

(Jesus & the Resurrection)
Jesus goes to Bethany and Jerusalem for Passover
Raises Lazarus ●
Resurrection and Life ◆
Anointed
Enters Jerusalem

● = Sign   ■ = Discourse   ◆ = "I AM" statement

THE BOOK OF GLORY

Jesus washes the disciples' feet

The Last Discourse ◆ ◆

Jesus prays for his disciples

Jesus is arrested and interrogated
Peter's denial

Jesus is put on trial

Jesus gives his life on the cross

Jesus rises from the dead and appears to his disciples

Epilogue

GEOGRAPHY OF THE GOSPEL OF JOHN

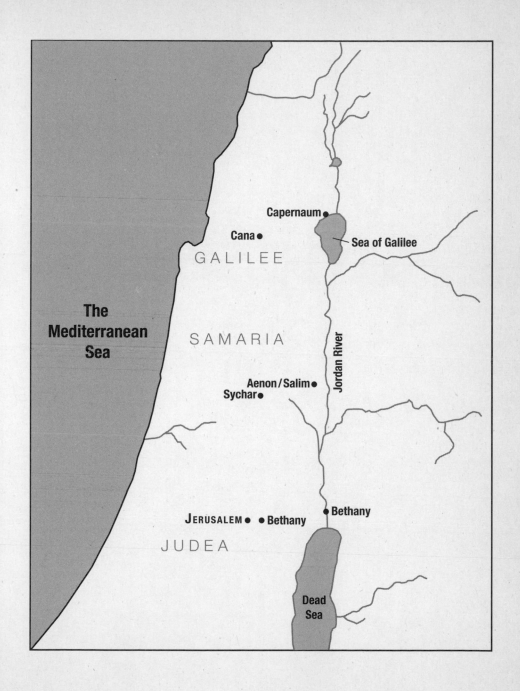

THE WORD OF GOD BECOMES FLESH

Gospel of John > Prologue

INTRODUCTION

If you go to the theater to see a musical like *Phantom of the Opera*, before the curtain rises and the action begins on stage, you'll hear an "overture" played by the orchestra. This overture will introduce you to the major song tunes. They'll probably be used in several places during the play. (If the play is made into a movie, the overture will likely accompany the opening credits.)

In the same way, before the action in the gospel of John begins, a poetic prologue introduces you to the major themes and ideas the book will consider. The prologue introduces these themes by giving special prominence to several key words. As you'll see in the weeks ahead, these words will be used repeatedly and significantly throughout the book as themes recur.

One way the prologue highlights words is by putting them at the end of one phrase and then repeating them at the beginning of the next phrase. For example (any italics in Scripture quotes throughout this book have been added):

In him was *life*,
and that *life* was the *light* of all people.
The *light* shines in the *darkness*,
and the *darkness* has not overcome it.

The prologue also highlights some important terms by drawing contrasts between them:

The law was given through *Moses*;
grace and truth came through *Jesus Christ*.

Whether or not you're conscious of the ways key terms are being highlighted, you'll find that certain specific words will stand out for you as you listen to the prologue.

⊃ Do you have any questions about this introduction?

⊃ Give some examples of musical movies or plays you've seen that have overtures.

READING

Have someone in your group read the prologue to the gospel of John out loud. It begins right at the start of the book, and it ends, "No one has ever seen God, but the one and only Son . . . has made him known."

As you listen, identify the key words that are highlighted by where they're used and how they're repeated. Jot them down during and after the reading.

Let one member of the group read their list of key words. Then go around the room and have others add words that haven't been mentioned yet. Make a list of all the words the group has identified. You can compare it with the suggested list in the "Notes" at the end of this session.

DISCUSSION

1 The central purpose of this book of the Bible is to show people how they can come into a living relationship with Jesus Christ. It was written by a man named John, who was one of Jesus' personal followers. He was especially close to him during his lifetime. John wanted everyone to come to know Jesus as he had. Near the end of the book, he explains that this was his purpose in writing: "These are written that you may believe that Jesus is the Messiah, the Son of God, and that by believing you may have life in his name." ("Messiah" is a name for the Savior sent by God.)

The words *believe* and *receive* in the prologue describe the fact of people coming into a relationship with Jesus. When people do this, they have *life*. They are *born* of God, who becomes their *Father*.

➲ Describe what your relationship with Jesus is right now, using key words from the prologue. (Anyone who isn't comfortable with this can pass.) You might say things like this:

- I haven't *received* Jesus yet, but I'm interested in finding out what difference he could make in my *life*.
- I have a lot of issues with calling God *"Father"* right now, but I do *believe* in Jesus.

2 Several other key words illustrate how people come into this relationship. The natural tendency of people in the *world* is to hide in *darkness*. When they do, they can't *understand* who Jesus is: "the world did not *recognize* him," "the darkness has not *understood* the light" (alternative translation). People must come into the *light* and acknowledge the *truth* about themselves. Then they'll also be able to recognize who Jesus is.

➲ What does "hiding in darkness" look like, in terms of how a person lives their life? How would this "hiding in darkness" keep a person from understanding who Jesus is?

3 Beyond its central purpose of introducing people to Jesus, the gospel of John has some other important themes. One of them is the question of *how followers of Jesus should relate to established religion*.

The book was probably written down during the last couple of decades in the first century (AD 80s–90s). At that time, the leaders of many Jewish synagogues in the Roman Empire were threatening to expel anyone who believed Jesus was the Messiah. This threat applied both to the Jews whose natural religious home was in the synagogue and to the many Gentiles who also worshipped there. Anyone who was expelled would lose their religious identity and be excluded from the special times and places where religious celebrations were held.

But even though the established religion is hostile and threatening, John insists that this shouldn't keep his readers from believing in Jesus. They will continue to possess everything that expulsion from the synagogue seems to take away, because *Jesus himself embodies the deepest meaning of these sacred times and places.* (For example, John will show that Jesus is the true temple, the true Sabbath, and so forth.)

In the prologue to the gospel of John, the idea of *grace in place of grace* points to this theme. So does the contrast between *Moses* and *Jesus Christ.* A similar contrast is drawn earlier between *his own* (the Jewish people, especially their religious leaders) and *all* (anyone, Jew or Gentile, who believes in Jesus).

➲ Describe how you currently relate to established religion. If someone isn't a part of established religion, what's the most valuable thing they're missing? Fellowship /community

4 Another important purpose of this book is to challenge the idea that following Jesus is mostly about the end of the world, or what happens to you when you die. John shows throughout the book that *a person who knows Jesus will experience eternal, transcendent realities right now, in this life.* They don't have to die and go to heaven to experience those realities, or wait for them to break into this world at the end of history.

In the prologue, the words *life* and *glory* point to these realities. The "eternal life" that Jesus gives doesn't just mean living on forever after you die; "eternal life" also means experiencing a new quality of life right now. Jesus' "glory" isn't just the splendor he has when he returns to rule the world. His "glory" is also the glimpses he gives of his intimate relationship and shared purpose with the Father. Some of the other key words we've already considered, such as *light* and *truth,* and being *born of God,* also point to the way that followers of Jesus, through their belief in him, are brought immediately into a new spiritual realm.

➲ Based on your own picture of "heaven," what aspects of heaven do you think a person can experience here on earth?
inner peace, comfort, God's love

⮌ Based on what you've discovered from the prologue, what are you looking forward to as your group studies the gospel of John?

FOR YOUR NEXT MEETING

Have someone read this explanation aloud to the rest of the group:

You may be used to reading and studying the Bible in small sections at a time. But the Bible is really a collection of writings that need to be experienced as a whole first, so that their parts can be understood meaningfully within their overall flow. (Would we try to discuss individual scenes from a movie without watching the whole thing first?) In our day, groups are rediscovering the power of reading the Scriptures out loud together at length. Most of the biblical writings are short enough that they can be read out loud within the time that groups usually take for one or two of their meetings.

The gospel of John has two main parts. The first part takes about an hour and twenty minutes to read out loud. Reading both parts together takes about two hours. Your group should decide whether it wants to read the first part, or both parts, at its next meeting. If necessary, arrange for a special meeting time to allow you to finish this reading and have a discussion afterwards. (If you're going to read the whole book, set up a break between the two parts.)

You might want to plan a meal or some special refreshments to enjoy after this reading, as the discussion will be more informal.

NOTES

A suggested list of key words in the prologue: Word, God, made, life, light, darkness, world, witness/testify, believe, receive, children, born, glory, Son, Father, grace, truth, law, Moses, Jesus Christ.

READING THE BOOK OF SIGNS

If your group has decided to read the entire gospel of John at this meeting, first do this session, during which you will read through the Book of Signs. Take a short break, and then do session 14, during which you will read through the Book of Glory. If you've decided to start by reading just the Book of Signs, do only session 2 at this meeting. You'll read the Book of Glory after you've done sessions 3 through 13, which are the individual studies for the Book of Signs.

To see the overall flow of these two parts (the Book of Signs and the Book of Glory) within the gospel of John, look at the outline on page 8.

INTRODUCTION

Have someone read this introduction aloud for the rest of the group:

The gospel of John has two main parts. The first part is often called the Book of Signs. It describes Jesus' public ministry. As it does, it relates seven "signs" or miracles that Jesus did. The second part of the gospel is known as the Book of Glory. It relates Jesus' private instructions to his disciples, and the story of his death and resurrection. (Jesus referred to his death as his "hour of glory.") The central themes of the gospel of John, which you discussed in session 1, run all the way through both parts.

The seven *signs* described in this first part of John aren't all the miracles that Jesus ever did. John tells us at the end of his book that Jesus did so many that it wouldn't be possible to relate them all. But these seven are chosen as representative of the kinds of miracles Jesus did. They are sufficient to disclose his *glory*. (The number seven in the Bible represents completeness.) You can see where Jesus performed each of these signs on the map on page 9.

The Book of Signs has seven *sections*, and these almost line up with the seven signs. Most sections contain one sign, and it comes near the beginning or end of the section. But one section has no sign, while another has two. This shows us that these sections are really created by a different principle. They actually describe seven *journeys* that Jesus takes. These journeys are usually to Judea, and primarily to Jerusalem for religious festivals. But in one case he travels across the Sea of Galilee instead. As we'll discover in the sessions ahead, the festivals and locations that Jesus visits allow his identity to be disclosed against the symbolic background of Jewish religious life and history. These are therefore journeys of discovery for the reader, who goes with Jesus to places where more truths about him are revealed.

There's another feature of the Book of Signs that allows us to recognize its sections: At the end of each section, John focuses on how people have, or have not, *believed* in Jesus.

In the Book of Signs there are also seven *discourses*. These are speeches that Jesus makes or long conversations he has with individuals or groups. Jesus needs to explain himself this way because people have difficulty *understanding* who he is and why he has come. These discourses appear mostly in the middle sections of the Book of Signs. In several cases the discourses interpret signs that Jesus has just performed.

As he's explaining who he is, Jesus makes seven "*I am*" statements. ("I AM" was a special name by which God was revealed in the Old Testament.) These statements identify him with a figure or symbol from Jewish religious history (for example, "I am the good shepherd"). Five of these statements appear in the Book of Signs, and two more appear in the Book of Glory.

As your group reads through the gospel of John, you can follow where the signs, discourses, and "I am" statements come within each section by looking at the outline on page 8.

READING

Have group members take turns as you read through the Book of Signs out loud. It begins right after the prologue with the sentence, "Now this was John's testimony when the Jewish leaders in Jerusalem sent priests and Levites to ask him who he was." It ends after Jesus enters Jerusalem and the crowd cries "Hosanna!" but the people don't truly believe in Jesus, despite all the signs he's done. In the last paragraph of the Book of Signs, Jesus says this:

"As for those who hear my words but do not keep them, I do not judge them. For I did not come to judge the world, but to save the world. There is a judge for those who reject me and do not accept my words; the very words I have spoken will condemn them at the last day. For I did not speak on my own, but the Father who sent me commanded me to say all that I have spoken. I know that his command leads to eternal life. So whatever I say is just what the Father has told me to say."

In *The Books of The Bible* there are several blank lines of space to mark the end of this major section.

This reading should take about an hour and twenty minutes. Change readers every time you come to one of the breaks indicated by white space in the text. (If you're not using *The Books of The Bible*, change readers when you come to the end of what seems like a scene of the story.)

When it's your turn to read, think of yourself as telling the story to the rest of the group. If you prefer not to read aloud, feel free to just let the next person take their turn.

As you hear the book read, you can use the map to see where the action is taking place, and you can follow the outline to see how the story is unfolding. Listen for how the major themes introduced in the prologue are being developed.

DISCUSSION

⮑ What was it like to hear a major portion of a gospel read out loud?

⮑ What things struck you most as you listened? What were your overall impressions?

IF YOU PLAN TO READ THE REST
OF THE GOSPEL NOW

If you plan to read the rest of the gospel of John at this meeting, take a break now, perhaps for some food, and then proceed with session 14 below.

THE FIRST SEVEN DAYS: JESUS MAKES DISCIPLES

**Gospel of John > Book of Signs >
First Section: Jesus as the New Creation**

INTRODUCTION

The first section of the Book of Signs describes the events of one week. John notes the passing of the days at the beginning of each episode, for example, "the next day," "on the third day." John portrays the opening of Jesus' ministry as one week to show symbolically that what Jesus is bringing to the world is so original, and that it will bring about such great changes, it's like a new creation. This symbolism comes from the book of Genesis, which describes the world being created over the course of one week.

This section fits the general pattern of describing a journey that Jesus takes, even though it begins in the middle of that journey. The section begins with Jesus already down in Judea, near **Bethany** on the east shore of the Jordan River. (This is not the same place as the village of Bethany near Jerusalem that's talked about later in the book.) A man named John the Baptist is calling people to be washed in the water of the river to show that they want to be cleansed from the wrong things they've done. At the end of the section, Jesus travels back up to **Galilee** to attend a wedding, where he turns water into wine. (That's why days five and six aren't described in detail; on those days, Jesus and his disciples are traveling from Judea back to Galilee.)

It's probably symbolically significant that this section begins and ends with references to water in the context of new beginnings and transformation, because in Genesis, the earth is formed out of water.

READING

Have five different members of your group read aloud what happens on each of the five days that are described in this section. The five days begin this way:

Day 1: "Now this was John's testimony . . ."

Day 2: "The next day John saw Jesus coming toward
him . . ."

Day 3: "The next day John was there again with two of his disciples
. . ."

Day 4: "The next day Jesus decided to leave for Galilee."

(Days 5 and 6 aren't described.)

Day 7: "On the third day a wedding took place . . ."

DISCUSSION

1 **Days 1 and 2: John the Baptist testifies to who Jesus is.** The "priests and Levites" who came to question John the Baptist were responsible for ceremonies of ritual cleansing. They wanted to know what authority he had to perform baptisms. Did he claim to be some kind of special messenger sent by God? John probably surprised them when he didn't insist on his own credentials (even though he really was sent by God). Instead, he claimed that ritual cleansing in water was actually insignificant compared with the transformation and new beginning that Jesus would bring. Jesus would "take away the sin of the world" and "baptize" (fill and surround) people with the Holy Spirit. This is an early expression of one of the main themes we've identified in the gospel of John: followers of Jesus will experience transcendent realities that religious ceremonies and institutions only point to. If you have Jesus, you have everything that ritual washing symbolizes: forgiveness for the wrong things you've done, a clean heart, a clear conscience, and a new beginning in life.

⮑ What ceremonies or observances are there in your culture that show a person has a "clean slate" and a new start in life?

⮑ (People can "pass" on these questions if they want:) Have you been baptized? If so, how, and at what age? What do you believe being baptized did for you? If you've had the opportunity to be baptized but have chosen not to, why have you made this choice?

⮑ Based on what John the Baptist both says and does, how would you answer someone today who said it wasn't important for them to be baptized because it's "only water"? (There's a suggested answer to this question at the end of this session that you can interact with after doing your own reflection.)

2 **Days 3 and 4: Jesus calls his first followers.** After hearing what John the Baptist says about Jesus, several of his disciples and their friends begin to understand more about who Jesus is. In the course of the first four days, they address Jesus by many different titles and describe him in ways that begin to reveal his identity.

⮑ Divide your group into four teams. Have each team look through days 1, 2, 3, and 4 in this section and identify all the titles and descriptions that are applied to Jesus. Have each team explain to the rest of the group what they think each title or description means. (Others in the group can help if the team isn't sure.) You can compare your lists with the suggested list at the end of this study.

◯ What title or description would you use to explain what Jesus means to you right now?

3 **Day 7: Jesus changes water to wine at a wedding in Cana.** Even after Jesus' followers understand all these things about him, they still don't "believe" or "put their faith" in him until the seventh day, when they attend a wedding feast with him. When the wine runs out, Jesus' mother Mary asks him for help. Jesus expects that the power of God will be increasingly demonstrated through him as his "hour" draws near (meaning the time of his death as the Savior of the world). But Mary's persistent faith and implicit trust show him that God is powerfully at work in this very moment. Jesus performs a miracle and transforms well over a hundred gallons of water into fine wine. This demonstrates God's concern to provide for material needs—even for celebrations. It also illustrates the joy and abundance God wants people to experience. This first sign reveals Jesus' "glory"—not so much his miraculous powers, but his intimate relationship with God and his sensitivity to the work God wants to do through him at each moment. This enables his disciples to understand, and *believe* in, who he really is.

◯ Have you ever had an experience where something you needed was provided in answer to faith and prayer, or in a surprising and unexpected way? If so, did this experience help you understand or believe something new about who God is? What was that something new?

NOTES

Suggested list of titles and descriptions of Jesus in the first section of the Book of Signs:

Day 1: the Lord; one you do not know; one whose sandals I am not worthy to untie.

Day 2: the Lamb of God who takes away the sins of the world; a man who comes after me; a man who surpasses me; a man who was before me; the one who will baptize with the Holy Spirit; God's Chosen One.

Day 3: the Lamb of God; Rabbi ("Teacher"); Messiah ("Christ," which means Anointed One).

Day 4: the one Moses and the prophets wrote about; Jesus of Nazareth, son of Joseph; Rabbi; Son of God; king of Israel; Son of Man.

Some thoughts on why someone who believes in Jesus should still be baptized, even if it's "only water": Throughout this gospel, Jesus uses "earthy things" as analogies to communicate the meaning of "heavenly things." (He'll explain this to Nicodemus in the reading for the next session.) Water is an "earthly thing," but being washed in water points to the "heavenly thing" of starting a new life by following Jesus. And this "earthly thing" is something we're not just supposed to look at, but be immersed in. In other words, the particular sign of baptism doesn't just give us a picture of something spiritual, it gives us a chance to express our commitment and involvement tangibly by involving ourselves physically in it.

JESUS CLEANSES THE TEMPLE AND SPEAKS WITH NICODEMUS

**Gospel of John > Book of Signs >
Second Section: Jesus and the Temple >
Trip to Jerusalem**

INTRODUCTION

The second section of the Book of Signs describes a journey that Jesus took from Galilee to Judea and back. Because of the length of this section, we'll take two sessions to consider it. In this session, we'll look at what happened in Jerusalem. In the next session, we'll look at what happened on Jesus' way back to Galilee. (When you read this section, you can find the locations mentioned on the map on page 9.)

Jesus traveled to Jerusalem on this occasion to attend the Passover festival. What's significant here is that Jesus goes to the *temple*. At the beginning of this section, and toward the end of it, Jesus' identity is examined in light of the purpose and significance of the temple. We'll start to consider this temple theme here, but look at it in detail in our next session.

Our primary concern in this session will be with the conversations Jesus has with the Jewish leaders at the temple and with Nicodemus. These are the first of the conversations that Jesus has with many different people in the gospel of John. These conversations tend to follow a pattern: Jesus speaks of spiritual realities, but his listeners misunderstand him and think he's speaking about material realities. They ask questions to try to clear up the confusion, and this gives Jesus (or John, speaking as the narrator) the opportunity to explain the spiritual realities further. In this section, John makes some comments after Jesus' conversation with Nicodemus, and he makes some more comments after telling us a little more about John the Baptist.

While the other gospel writers describe Jesus cleansing the temple at the end of his ministry, John tells the story now because of the themes he wants to develop. John isn't necessarily writing a strictly chronological account; he's telling us about Jesus in a way that will help us understand who he is, and believe.

READING

Read the three episodes in this section out loud like a play. (You can leave out cues like "Jesus answered," "they responded," "Nicodemus asked," etc.) Have different group members read the parts that are listed.

Jesus cleanses the temple. (This episode begins, "When it was almost time for the Jewish Passover, Jesus went up to Jerusalem.")
Narrator
Jesus
Jewish leaders

The conversation between Jesus and Nicodemus. (It begins, "Now there was a Pharisee, a man named Nicodemus . . .")
Narrator
Jesus
Nicodemus

The further story of John the Baptist. (It begins "After this, Jesus and his disciples went out . . ." It ends, ". . . but whoever rejects the Son will not see life, for God's wrath remains on them.")
Narrator
John the Baptist's disciples
John the Baptist

DISCUSSION

1 A certain amount of commerce was necessary to support the operations of the temple in Jerusalem. Worshippers needed to buy animals to offer in sacrifice. They also needed to exchange their Roman coins for other coins that wouldn't be offensive within the temple (since Roman coins called the emperor a god). In Jesus' time, all of this commerce had moved right into the temple court, which should have been reserved for worship instead.

Jesus, always sensitive to his Father's heart in any situation, is filled with indignation when he sees this. He drives out the merchants, yelling, "Stop turning my Father's house into a market!" Earlier the Jewish leaders demanded to know by what authority John baptized; now they ask Jesus what authority he has to say what can happen in the temple. Is he claiming to be the figure that the prophets predicted would come and purify the temple? If so, can he perform some sign or miracle to prove his identity?

Jesus says he will give them a sign: If they destroy the "temple," he will "raise it again" in three days. The leaders think he's speaking on a material level about the huge temple building. But John explains that Jesus is speaking on a spiritual level, about the "temple" of his body.

➲ Picture Jesus, dressed in a way that's typical for your culture, attending your church this week. (If you don't go to church regularly, think of a church you may have visited.) How does Jesus feel about the various things he sees and hears, as he senses with the heart of God?

➲ What are some of the things that people would say a visitor (like Jesus, if they didn't recognize him) has "no right" to question?

2 John tells us that when Jesus was in Jerusalem for Passover, he performed numerous "signs." (In his book John only describes seven signs, but he reports many others in places like this.) Many people came to have a superficial, unreliable belief in Jesus based on what they thought were demonstrations of power and authority.

Nicodemus provides a specific example of this kind of person. He comes to visit Jesus and congratulates him on being "a teacher sent from God." He explains that he's figured out who Jesus is based on the signs he's done. The implication is that Nicodemus wants to hear more of Jesus' ideas. Jesus recognizes that Nicodemus wants "in," but he has to explain to him what being "in" really means. It means becoming part of the realm of heaven-on-earth, which Jesus is introducing. To enter this realm and have his true origin from heaven, Nicodemus needs to be "born again" (or "born from above").

Nicodemus misunderstands the phrase to mean "born a second time." When he protests that this is physically impossible, Jesus explains that he's actually talking about a spiritual birth.

We'll meet Nicodemus twice more, later in the book, as he continues to grapple with the identity of Jesus and he finally takes a stand for him.

⮑ Have you experienced a spiritual rebirth through Jesus? If so, how did this happen? If not, do you think a spiritual rebirth is possible? If it is possible, how do you think it would happen?

3 The argument that John the Baptist's disciples had with "a certain Jew" probably arose when they were challenged to explain why people should still come to John to be baptized, rather than to Jesus and his disciples, since John had already said that Jesus was much greater than he was. This questioner seems to represent the general attitude of the people, who were now turning to Jesus. In response, John the Baptist compares himself to the best man at a wedding, whose own joy comes from seeing his friend "get the bride."

⮑ John the Baptist says about Jesus, "He must become greater; I must become less." If you took this statement as your own motto, what's the first place where this would make a difference in your life?

4 After the conversation with Nicodemus, and again after the report about John the Baptist at **Aenon**, John the narrator explains more about the spiritual realities Jesus has been describing. He uses many of the key words and concepts that were introduced in the prologue. These appear in many places throughout the book, but here in John's comments (and in Jesus' conversation with Nicodemus) they are densely packed together, and they help interpret one another.

⮑ Work together as a group to create a sentence that demonstrates the relationship among the following key words from the prologue, as their relationship is explained in John's comments here:

truth, light, darkness

⮑ Do the same for these key words:

world, life, God, believe

⮑ People often use the phrase "eternal life" to mean living forever in heaven after you die. But John says here that "whoever believes in the Son has eternal life" already. What does it mean to have "eternal life" right now?

JESUS SPEAKS WITH A SAMARITAN WOMAN AND HEALS AN OFFICIAL'S SON

**Gospel of John > Book of Signs >
Second Section: Jesus and the Temple >
Return to Galilee**

INTRODUCTION

The rest of this section in the Book of Signs describes Jesus' return to Galilee from Judea. On his way back home, he meets a woman in the village of **Sychar** in **Samaria**. (You can locate this village on the map on page 9.)

Jesus has a conversation with this woman that's much like the conversation he had with Nicodemus, which we looked at in session 4. Jesus speaks to her of spiritual realities, but she misunderstands and thinks he's speaking about material realities. But her questions allow him to explain these spiritual realities further. Their conversation leads into a deeper exploration of the meaning of the temple, and of Jesus' identity against the backdrop of the temple.

Once Jesus has returned to the village of **Cana** in Galilee, a royal official asks him to heal his son. Jesus is concerned that the official may only want to see a demonstration of power. As we saw in session 4, Jesus doesn't want to encourage superficial faith based on miracles. (John tells us that many Galileans saw the signs Jesus did at Passover, as did Nicodemus and others in Jerusalem.)

But when the official, like Mary at the wedding feast earlier, shows persistent faith and trust, Jesus recognizes that God is at work in the situation. It becomes the occasion for the second "sign" that John describes in detail. This section ends with a description of how the royal official, like the woman and her neighbors in the Samaritan village, came to *believe* in Jesus.

READING

Read the stories of Jesus' conversation with the Samaritan woman and the healing of the royal official's son. Assign parts to different speakers and read these episodes out loud like a play.

 Jesus and the Samaritan woman. (It begins, "Now Jesus learned that the Pharisees . . .")
> Narrator
> Jesus
> Samaritan woman
> Jesus' disciples
> Samaritan villagers

 Jesus and the royal official. (It begins, "After the two days he left for Galilee . . ." It ends, "This was the second sign Jesus performed after coming from Judea to Galilee.")
> Narrator
> Jesus
> royal official
> his servants

DISCUSSION

1 The conversation between Jesus and the Samaritan woman begins on a material level. Jesus is tired and thirsty, and he simply asks her for a drink. The woman, however, immediately mentions their religious differences as a problem. Jews considered Samaritans "unclean" and wouldn't share cups or bowls with them. The woman can't believe that Jesus doesn't feel constrained by these ritual practices.

With this opening, Jesus then speaks on a spiritual level of the "living water" the woman can receive from God, even though she's a Samaritan. The woman misunderstands him to be speaking about "flowing water," which would be cooler and fresher than what she can get from this well. When she asks how she can get this water, Jesus explains that he's referring to an internal spiritual reality that leads to "eternal life."

(Later in the book, when Jesus speaks similarly of "rivers of living water" flowing within those who believe, John explains that Jesus is referring to "the Spirit.")

➲ Jesus tells the Samaritan woman that he's the one who gives the "living water." In your understanding and experience, how does someone who believes in Jesus receive the Holy Spirit that he gives? What is the "thirst" that the Spirit continually quenches?

2 When the woman asks for the "living water," Jesus challenges her first to "come into the light" (as the gospel of John often puts it) and acknowledge the wrong way she's been living. When Jesus asks about her husband, she gives a factually true but misleading answer. But when Jesus reveals the facts of the woman's life, she admits that what he's said about her is true.

(This is one example of the "irony" that often occurs in the book: people say things that are truer than they admit, or truer than they realize. Another example is when the woman wonders aloud whether Jesus is greater than Jacob. Actually, he is.)

It seems that she does receive eternal life in the end. When she goes to tell the rest of the villagers about Jesus, she leaves her water jar behind. When John includes specific details like this, they're significant. It's not that the woman is in such a hurry that she forgets the jar. She doesn't need it any more. She's got living water inside her.

➲ (For group discussion) The Samaritan woman was able to confess privately to Jesus how she'd been living. She received forgiveness and began a new life. Where can people today go to confess openly to another person, but privately and in confidence, so that they give up their wrong ways of life and begin living in a new way?

⊃ (For private reflection) Is there something in your life that you've been describing to others in a misleading way? Does this indicate that you need to make a change in your life?

3 When the Samaritan woman recognizes that Jesus is a reliable prophet, she asks him to settle a contentious question of her day: where is the right place for people to go to worship God? In response to her genuine spiritual searching, Jesus answers that it's not *where* we go that matters, but *how* we go. God is looking for people from every background to come and worship "in Spirit and in truth." This echoes the theme that was introduced when Jesus cleansed the temple. We don't need to go to a temple or sanctuary to enter into the presence of God. If you're with Jesus, you're already in the presence of God. Jesus himself is the true temple, the dwelling place of God on earth.

⊃ What does it mean to worship in "Spirit" and in "truth"? To help answer this question, define what the opposite would be. (For example, what does false or fake worship look like?)

4 The healing of the official's son illustrates the truth of what Jesus told the Samaritan woman, about God seeking people from everywhere as worshippers. The official was a Gentile, even further removed from the people of Israel than the Samaritans. But like the Samaritans in the woman's village, he comes to a genuine faith in Jesus as the "Savior of the world."

⊃ Work together as a group to retell the episode of the healing of the royal official's servant from the perspective of one of his servants who comes to meet him on the road. (Someone with a laptop can record and edit the story as you develop it. Some members of the group may be able to illustrate your story with drawings or sketches.)

JESUS HEALS A MAN WHO COULDN'T WALK AND DEFENDS WORKING ON THE SABBATH

Gospel of John > Book of Signs >
Third Section: Jesus and the Sabbath

INTRODUCTION

The third section of the Book of Signs describes a journey that Jesus took to **Jerusalem** for another festival. John doesn't specify which festival, because the focus of this section is not on the festival itself. The focus is on the Sabbath, the seventh day of the week, when Jews weren't supposed to work, and the controversy Jesus had with the Jewish leaders in Jerusalem about it.

It's implied that Jesus returned to Galilee after this festival, because he's back there at the start of the next section. This section, like the others, ends with a reference to believing in Jesus, but in this case it's a description of how people failed to *believe*.

READING

Read aloud the story of Jesus healing the man who couldn't walk, and the account of the dispute he had afterward with the Jewish leaders. Have three different members of your group read this section in these three parts:

The account of the healing. (It begins, "Some time later, Jesus went up to Jerusalem . . .")

 Jesus' explanation to the Jewish leaders about working on the Sabbath. (It begins, "So, because Jesus was doing these things on the Sabbath . . .")

 Jesus' description to the Jewish leaders of the witnesses who testify for him. (It begins, "If I testify about myself . . ." It ends, "But since you do not believe what he wrote, how are you going to believe what I say?")

DISCUSSION

1 The dispute between Jesus and the Jewish leaders is another discourse (speech or conversation) in the gospel of John, like the ones with Nicodemus and the Samaritan woman.) This discourse interprets a sign that Jesus has just performed, as some later discourses will do.

The man by the pool isn't just disabled, he's unmotivated. Jesus can tell by looking at him that he's been there a long time. (Perhaps he's made himself really comfortable?) Jesus asks if he even *wants* to be healed. In reply, the man offers an excuse for why he can't be.

But Jesus heals him, and transforms him from someone who's been very conspicuously doing nothing to someone who's "working"—on the Sabbath. (Carrying a sleeping mat was defined as work.)

This sign therefore discloses something about Jesus' identity: Jesus is the one who makes it possible to "work on the Sabbath," in a particular sense. The Jews of Jesus' day already accepted that God had to be at work sometimes on the Sabbath. They believed, for example, that God actively sent rain, and it often rained on the Sabbath. But human work was forbidden. Jesus explained, however, that the work he was doing was not his own, but the Father's. "The Son can do nothing by himself; he can only do what he sees his Father doing, because whatever the Father does the Son also does."

This is actually a good description of Jesus' "glory": his intimate relationship with the Father and his sensitivity to the work that the Father wants to do through him at any given moment. The point is that followers of Jesus can have this same kind of relationship with the Father and be actively involved in God's own work on every single day of the week.

> ⊃ How can we identify work that God is already doing and wants us to be a part of personally?

> ⊃ What excuses might we give for being unmotivated, like the man by the pool, and not joining God in his work or even recognizing it?

2 Jesus explains that the work the Father has given him to do includes giving "eternal life" to all who believe in him, and judging those who refuse to believe. Both of these things are present spiritual realities. Jesus says that his followers already *have* eternal life, and that the time *has now come* when the dead will hear his voice and live.

This is another expression of a recurring theme we've identified: following Jesus isn't just about what happens when you die or at the end of the world. (John also comments, for example, after Jesus' conversation with Nicodemus, that "whoever does not believe stands condemned *already*," and Jesus tells the Samaritan woman that "a time is coming, *and has now come*, when the true worshippers will worship the Father in the Spirit and in truth.")

But Jesus' powers to judge and to give life are also a future physical reality. He says that "a time is coming when all who are in their graves will hear his voice and come out—those who have done what is good will rise to live, and those who have done what is evil will rise to be condemned." The present and future aspects of Jesus' work are stressed equally in the gospel of John.

> ⊃ Those who will hear Jesus' voice in the future will be physically dead ("in their graves"). Those who can hear Jesus' voice now are spiritually dead. What's a person like who is spiritually dead? What's a person like who is spiritually alive? (Describe the differences between them.)

3 Jesus' claims about his relationship with the Father, and about the honors and privileges the Father has given him, are so extraordinary that he knows the Jewish leaders won't accept them on his word alone. And so he cites four witnesses who "testify" on his behalf: John the Baptist, his own works, the Father, and the Scriptures.

⊃ At this time in your life, which of the following (if any) gives you the greatest confidence that Jesus is who he said he was?

a. What other people have told you about Jesus.

b. The things you've seen Jesus do in your life and in others' lives.

c. The assurance God gives you in your heart.

d. What the Bible says about Jesus.

FOR YOUR NEXT MEETING

In the next session we'll look at how Jesus fed the crowds who came to hear him teach, and how he gathered up the food that was left over so it wouldn't be wasted. Your group will be invited to share your own food with others in need. Have each member plan to bring a box or can of nonperishable food that the group can donate to a local food pantry. Also, if your group doesn't regularly meet for a meal in connection with your study, you might want to arrange to have a meal together for the next session.

JESUS BY THE SEA OF GALILEE:
THE BREAD OF LIFE

**Gospel of John > Book of Signs >
Fourth Section: Jesus and the Exodus**

INTRODUCTION

The fourth section of the Book of Signs describes a journey that Jesus takes across the **Sea of Galilee** and back. The action occurs at the time of Passover. But in this section Jesus' identity is still not explored against the background of that festival. (This will happen in the Book of Glory.)

Instead, the focus is on understanding Jesus' identity against the background of the event that Passover commemorates: the *exodus* of the people of Israel from Egypt under the leadership of Moses. While Jesus is on the far shore of the lake, he miraculously feeds a large crowd. When the crowd returns to the opposite shore, they compare this feeding with the manna, the "bread from heaven," that Moses gave the Israelites in the wilderness. And to get back across the lake, Jesus miraculously walks on the water. This recalls the way God made a path through the Red Sea so the Israelites could escape from the Egyptians. The two "signs" that Jesus does at the beginning of this section thus associate him with the exodus.

Moses was not just the Israelites' leader, he was also their teacher. He explained to them, God "humbled you, causing you to hunger and then feeding you with manna . . . to teach you that people do not live on bread alone but on every word that comes from the mouth of the LORD." In a long discourse that interprets the meaning of the miraculous feeding, Jesus explains that he is himself the true "bread from heaven." Whoever comes to Jesus, hearing his message and believing in him, will have eternal life. "I am the bread of life," he declares. In light of Moses and the exodus, Jesus is seen as the greater leader and teacher of the people of Israel. But he is also the ultimate embodiment of the gift that God gave through Moses: the "bread that comes down from heaven and gives life to the world."

At the end of this section, many of those who've been following Jesus turn away from him because of his challenging words. But John also describes how his closest disciples reaffirm what they've come to *believe* about him. "You have the words of eternal life," Peter affirms, "you are the Holy One of God."

READING

Read the fourth section of the Book of Signs like a play. Have different members take different parts in its three episodes (you can leave out cues like "they asked," "Jesus answered," etc.):

 The miraculous feeding. (It begins, "Some time after this, Jesus crossed to the far shore of the Sea of Galilee . . .")
    Narrator
    Jesus
    Philip
    Andrew
    the crowd

 Jesus walks on the water. (It begins, "When evening came, his disciples went down to the lake . . .")
    Narrator
    Jesus

Discourse on the bread of life. (It begins, "The next day the crowd that had stayed . . ." It ends, "He meant Judas, the son of Simon Iscariot, who, though one of the Twelve, was later to betray him.")

Narrator

Jesus

the crowd

the Jewish leaders

the disciples who stop following Jesus

Peter

DISCUSSION

1 As we've seen earlier in the book of John, Jesus was careful not to encourage a superficial faith based on miraculous signs that were understood as demonstrations of power and authority. In this section, he recognizes that the crowd's interest in him, which was originally based on such a superficial faith, has come to be motivated by something even worse: the desire for another free lunch! (The crowd wants a continuing supply of free food to be the next "sign" that Jesus does so that they'll believe in him.)

The discourse that follows the miraculous feeding explains its meaning. In this discourse, Jesus turns the crowd's focus from the sign itself to what it reveals about who he is. He wants the people to see him not as the one who *gave* the bread, but as the one who *is* the bread. His identification of himself with the manna, the "bread from heaven," points to his heavenly origins and the divine life he imparts.

⊃ Have you ever wanted to see a miracle for any of these reasons?

    a. I want God to do something miraculous for me, because there are things I want and need that I can't get for myself.

    b. I want God to do something miraculous to prove he exists, so I will believe in him.

    c. I want God to give me a sign that reveals something about who he is.

⊃ Have you ever received a "sign" from God that did show you something more about who God is? If so, what happened, and what did you learn?

2 Many interpreters believe that Jesus' words here about "eating his flesh" and "drinking his blood" are a reference to the Lord's Supper (or "Eucharist"). These interpreters point out that John doesn't describe anywhere else in his gospel how Jesus instituted this sacrament. They suggest that John may therefore be doing that here. Eucharistic themes do run through the gospel. For example, the two things that Jesus provides miraculously are wine (at the wedding in Cana) and bread (on the far shore of the Sea of Galilee).

⊃ If you regularly attend a worship gathering of Jesus' followers, share with the group how your community celebrates the Lord's Supper. Is it a full meal, or symbolic portions of bread and wine or juice? Are the elements passed around on plates and trays, or do people come forward to receive them, or is everyone seated at a table? Do people need to be qualified in some way to take part? For example, do they need to have been baptized, or do they need to believe something specific about how the Lord's Supper works?

⊃ What's one of the most meaningful experiences you've ever had of receiving the Lord's Supper or Eucharist?

⊃ At the end of session 6, you were asked to bring nonperishable food for the poor to this meeting. Decide as a group where you will donate the food you've collected, and who will deliver it. Have them give a brief report about the delivery at the start of session 8.

JESUS DECLARES HE'S THE SOURCE OF LIVING WATER

**Gospel of John > Book of Signs >
Fifth Section: Jesus and the Festival of Tabernacles > First
Discourse**

INTRODUCTION

The fifth section of the Book of Signs describes a journey that Jesus takes to **Jerusalem** to attend the Festival of Tabernacles. While he is there, his identity is explored against the background of that festival. By appealing to its history and symbolism, and by doing a further sign, Jesus shows more about who he is.

At the festival, Jesus reveals himself through three long discourses with the Jewish leaders and the crowds. (These are the last three of the seven in the Book of Signs.) Because this section is so long, we'll devote three sessions to it. We'll look at one of these discourses in each session.

Jesus' miracles and teaching have caused so much controversy that, before he can present himself positively to the people, he needs to clear up some misunderstandings and false accusations. That's what he does in this first discourse. But after addressing these misunderstandings, Jesus also begins to disclose his identity through the symbolism of the Festival of Tabernacles.

This festival commemorated the way the Israelites lived in tents as God led them through the wilderness to the Promised Land. But Tabernacles was also an agricultural festival. It included prayers for rain for the coming year's crops. The people appealed to God to send them rain, just as he had made water flow from a rock for the Israelites in the wilderness. And so when Jesus calls out, "Let anyone who is thirsty come to me and drink," he's claiming that he embodies the life-giving water of Israel's history.

But Jesus' words in this discourse also have a future aspect. The last prophecy recorded in the book of Zechariah foretells a time when "living water" will flow continually out of Jerusalem. This is associated with a world-wide celebration of the Feast of Tabernacles. Thus, when Jesus promises that "rivers of living water" will flow within anyone who believes in him, he's also claiming that he embodies the life-giving water of Israel's future expectation.

READING

This first discourse at the Feast of Tabernacles is made up of four conversations. Have four members of your group read them aloud:

 Conversation 1: Jesus speaks with his brothers about attending the festival. (It begins, "After this, Jesus went around in Galilee.")

 Conversation 2: Jesus teaches at the festival and explains he's not a Sabbath-breaker. (It begins, "Not until halfway through the festival did Jesus go up to the temple courts . . .")

 Conversation 3: Jesus answers the claim that he can't be the Messiah if people know where he's from. (It begins, "At that point, some of the people in Jerusalem began to ask, 'Isn't this the man they are trying to kill?'")

 Conversation 4: Jesus offers the living water, and people respond in different ways. (It begins, "On the last and greatest day of the festival . . ." and ends, "a prophet does not come out of Galilee.")

DISCUSSION

1 We saw back in session 6 how Jesus healed an invalid on the Sabbath. He told the Jewish leaders he was doing God's work on that day. They were so infuriated that they wanted to kill him. So Jesus has been staying away from Jerusalem.

But now he has an important opportunity to reveal more about who he is through the symbolism of the Festival of Tabernacles. (We'll learn even more about this symbolism in our next two sessions.) Jesus decides to attend the festival, but secretly, not just for safety's sake, but also because he's not seeking personal glory for himself.

His brothers take this as one more reason not to believe he's really the Messiah. They reason that if Jesus knows he's meant to be a "public figure," he should be at this festival, trying to draw some attention to himself, since Jews from all over the world will attend. "Reveal yourself to the world," Jesus' brothers urge him. This is ironic, since Jesus has been revealing himself by seeking the Father's glory instead of his own.

➲ In the 1970s rock opera Jesus Christ Superstar, Tim Rice and Andrew Lloyd Webber ask Jesus, "Why'd you choose such a backward time and such a strange land? If you'd come today, you could have reached the whole nation. Israel in 4 BC had no mass communication." How do you think Jesus would answer this question?

2 The crowds at the festival have heard a lot about Jesus. Because he has healed the sick and fed the hungry, some conclude that he's a "good man." Others object that he worked on the Sabbath by healing a man, and so he's leading the people astray by encouraging them not to keep the Law.

When Jesus begins to teach publicly at the festival, he addresses this objection directly. He demonstrates that his accusers don't keep the Law themselves the way they expect him to. The Sabbath, even to his accusers, is not an absolute prohibition of work. There are certain activities they will carry out, such as circumcision, if the eighth day after a boy's birth falls on the

Sabbath. If they can justify doing this kind of work, then certainly healing is even more justified.

⮑ Put Jesus on trial for breaking the law. Choose members from your group to be the judge, prosecuting attorney, and defense attorney. Let the attorneys decide what witnesses they want to call, and have group members play the parts of these witnesses. (For example, the attorneys might call the man who was healed, parents whose child's circumcision day fell on a Sabbath, a *moel* or ritual circumciser who has performed the ceremony on a Sabbath, Pharisees who consider themselves experts on the law, Jesus himself, and so forth.)

The rest of the group members can serve as the jury. They must return a verdict of "guilty" or "not guilty" based on whether they believe the charges have been proven beyond a reasonable doubt. (There will be no eternal consequences if the jury, after deliberating the evidence presented, votes "guilty.")

3 Many in the time of Jesus expected that the Messiah would appear suddenly, as if from nowhere, with mystery surrounding his origins. Since they knew where Jesus was from, they concluded he couldn't be the Messiah. In response, Jesus says that they might think they know *where* he's from, but they don't know *who* he's from, and they don't know where he's *going*.

Jesus means that the crowds, thinking only of what they know about his earthly origins, don't recognize him as the one who has descended to earth from heaven and who will ascend there again. (In this way Jesus is like the person he told Nicodemus about, a person who is "born of the Spirit" and is like the wind: "you cannot tell where it comes from or where it is going.")

⮑ Celebrities today often create new identities for themselves that conceal their ordinary backgrounds. As a result, it seems that in a sense they have appeared out of nowhere. For example, they might change their names, change their appearance, move to a new region or country, and even adopt a different language. What examples can you provide of celebrities doing this sort of thing?

➲ In what ways do we give Jesus this kind of "makeover" in the ways we think about him and picture him? How can our pictures of Jesus reflect both his heavenly origins and the reality of his coming to earth?

4 When Jesus promises "rivers of living water" to anyone who believes in him, many in the crowd recognize that he has been sent from God. But others refuse to believe because they still can't get past the objections they have to what he's saying and doing.

➲ Complete one of the following sentences:

a. The main thing I had to "get past" so I could become a follower of Jesus was . . .

b. I might want to follow Jesus someday, but I still can't get past . . .

c. In my culture, the main thing that people need to get past in order to follow Jesus is . . .

FOR YOUR NEXT MEETING

The story of the woman who was caught in adultery probably preserves a genuine episode from the life of Jesus, but it was most likely not an original part of the gospel of John, so we didn't consider it in this study. However, your group may want to read it and discuss it, perhaps over dinner before doing session 9.

JESUS DECLARES HE'S THE LIGHT OF THE WORLD

Gospel of John > Book of Signs >
Fifth Section: Jesus and the Festival of Tabernacles >
Second Discourse

INTRODUCTION

Jesus wants to continue revealing his identity against the backdrop of the Festival of Tabernacles. So he introduces the theme of *light*, which is another vital symbol in the festival. But before he can develop this theme, his opponents raise more objections that he must address. As he pleads urgently with them to believe in him while there's still time, they misunderstand his words, and he has to correct these misunderstandings in order to explain the spiritual realities he's really speaking about. All of this generates a second extended discourse among Jesus, the Jewish leaders, and the crowds who are in Jerusalem for the festival.

READING

Read aloud the next discourse at the Festival of Tabernacles. This discourse has three parts. You'll need a pair of readers for each part, one to read Jesus' words and one to read what the crowd says in response to Jesus. (You can leave out cues like "the Pharisees challenged him," "Jesus answered," etc.) In addition, you'll need a reader for the short narrative that ends each part.

 The Pharisees object that Jesus is serving as his own witness. (It begins, "When Jesus spoke again to the people, he said, 'I am the light of the world.'")

    Jesus

    Pharisees

    Narrator ("He spoke these words while teaching in the temple courts . . .")

 Jesus speaks of his own death and urges the people to believe in him. ("Once more Jesus said to them, 'I am going away . . .'")

    Jesus

    the crowd

    Narrator ("They did not understand that he was telling them . . .")

 Jesus warns that being a physical descendant of Abraham doesn't automatically convey spiritual privileges. (It begins, "To the Jews who had believed him, Jesus said . . .")

    Jesus

    the crowd

    Narrator ("At this, they picked up stones to stone him . . .")

DISCUSSION

1 We saw in session 6 that when Jesus was challenged after he healed the man who couldn't walk, he cited four witnesses who testified in his favor. But here, when the Pharisees dispute Jesus' claim that he's the "light of the world," he tells them he doesn't actually need any other witnesses, because of where he comes from and where he's going. He means that his close relationship with the Father who sent him into the world ensures that he always speaks the truth. (His father, in fact, *can* be understood as a witness for him.) If the Pharisees knew who he or his Father really were, they'd know he was truthful. Jesus never misrepresents himself, because he always walks in the light.

⮑ Jesus' words here remind us that we can sometimes accept a person's word because of their character, even without proof or corroboration. Is there someone in your life whose word you would trust implicitly? What qualities does this person have that allow you to trust them? In what way do they "walk in the light"?

⮑ Have you had an experience where you were challenged to trust God without having a guarantee of how things would turn out? How did you respond? What happened in the end?

2 Jesus then speaks of his own impending death, and pleads with the people to believe in him while there's still time. They misunderstand what he means by "where I go, you cannot come," and so he explains that he will be returning "above."

When Jesus says, "If you do not believe that I AM . . . you will indeed die in your sins," he's applying a special name of God to himself. But the people once again misunderstand, and ask, "Who are you?" ("Who are we supposed to believe you are?")

He replies that when he is "lifted up" (meaning his death on the cross and his return to God's presence), "you will know that I AM." When the people finally recognize he's identifying himself with his heavenly Father and explaining his perfect obedience to the Father's will, many of them do believe in him.

⮑ In this part of the discourse, and also in the following part, Jesus appeals to the principle that "children do what their parents do." (As we say today, "like father, like son," or "the apple doesn't fall far from the tree.") This principle is illustrated perfectly in Jesus' own life: as he says earlier in the book, "whatever the Father does the Son does also." Do you feel that you're becoming God's spiritual child to a greater and greater extent? If so, are you seeing your character transformed and your behavior changing? In what ways is this happening?

3 Jesus promises that if anyone who believes in him holds to his teaching, they'll know the truth and it will set them free. (The people asked about the truth at the beginning of this discourse.)

Jesus is talking about spiritual freedom. But once again the people misunderstand. They think he's talking about freedom from civil or political servitude. As descendants of Abraham, they believe they've always been part of the "great nation" God promised would come from Abraham. They don't think they've ever really been subject to another earthly power. Jesus has to explain that he's talking about spiritual slavery to sin. He also insists that Abraham isn't really their father, because if they were genuinely his children, they would respond to Jesus the way Abraham did. Their behavior in rejecting and threatening Jesus suggests that their father is instead the devil, who is a liar and a murderer. This is one of the sharpest exchanges in the whole gospel of John.

When Jesus promises that anyone who follows him will never see death, the people misunderstand him once more. They think he's talking about physical death. They protest that the greatest figures in their religious history (such as Abraham and the prophets) all died physically. So who does he think he is?

When Jesus asserts that he existed before Abraham, and he once more uses the divine name I AM to describe himself, his opponents finally understand that he's claiming to be God. But since they don't believe his claim, they consider him guilty of blasphemy.

⮡ Here in the middle of the Book of Signs, we see Jesus going to great lengths to address the confusion and conflict he's been encountering. As he corrects misunderstandings and challenges resistance, he offers some very clear statements that concisely express his identity and mission. Which of the following statements, taken from this discourse, is most meaningful to you right now? Why? How would you restate it in your own words?

a. "I am the light of the world. Whoever follows me will never walk in darkness, but will have the light of life."

b. "A slave has no permanent place in the family, but a son belongs to it forever. So if the Son sets you free, you will be free indeed."

c. "If you hold to my teaching, you are really my disciples. Then you will know the truth, and the truth will set you free."

d. (Some other statement in the discourse.)

JESUS HEALS A BLIND MAN AND DECLARES HE'S THE GOOD SHEPHERD

**Gospel of John > Book of Signs >
Fifth Section: Jesus and the Festival of Tabernacles >
Third Discourse**

INTRODUCTION

When Jesus declared, "I am the light of the world," this claim met with so much resistance that he couldn't explain it further at the time. So now he does a sign that illustrates this aspect of his identity. He heals a man who was blind from birth. As he does, he says again, "I am the light of the world," still seeking to disclose his identity through the imagery of the Festival of Tabernacles.

This festival recalled how God led the Israelites through the wilderness. God went ahead of them, lighting the way at night, as a "pillar of fire." So the festival looked back to a great light of the past. But it also looked forward to a future light. We saw in session 8 that the final prophecy in the book of Zechariah describes a future worldwide observance of the Feast of Tabernacles and speaks of "living water" flowing from Jerusalem. This same prophecy also predicts that "on that day" there will be "no distinction between day and night." Even "when evening comes, there will be light." In keeping with this emphasis on past and future supernatural light, during the festival bright lights were lit in the temple courts near the place where the offerings were put.

Jesus was in that exact spot when he first declared that he was the light of the world. So, in the context of the festival, he's the past light, he's the future light, and he's the current reality of spiritual light. (When Jesus explains who he is like this against the background of Jewish religion, history, and culture, there are often past, future, and present references like this.)

But when Jesus heals the blind man to signify that he's the "light of the world," this happens on the Sabbath. And Jesus heals him by working: making mud. (This may have represented a re-creation of the man's eyes, since the book of Genesis describes people being formed from the "dust of the earth.") The healing causes so much controversy that it generates one more long discourse. This gives Jesus the opportunity to describe himself by one more image from Israel's religious heritage, the good shepherd.

At the end of this fifth section in the Book of Signs, there's once again a report about people *believing* (or not believing) in Jesus. In this case, it's a description of the sharply divided opinions about him.

READING

Have a member of your group who has good dramatic expression read the story of Jesus healing the man born blind, and the series of conversations that's sparked by the story. While this person is reading, have other members of the group silently act out the episode.

The story begins, "As he went along, he saw a man blind from birth." It ends, "But others said, 'These are not the sayings of someone possessed by a demon. Can a demon open the eyes of the blind?'" (If you have a Bible with chapter numbers, ignore the break between chapters 9 and 10. The discourse continues well into chapter 10.)

You'll need people to take these parts in the silent play:

Jesus
his disciples
the man born blind
the man's neighbors
the Pharisees
the man's parents

Begin with the man sitting and begging in the middle of the room. Have Jesus and his disciples walk up to him. Have the blind man go away to the "Pool of Siloam" and return. Have his neighbors bring him to the Pharisees (in a corner of the room). And so forth. When the reader is reading a character's lines, the person who's playing that character can gesture with their hands, shrug, shake their finger accusingly, etc.

DISCUSSION

1 Jesus' disciples don't think it's fair that this man has suffered blindness since birth. They're puzzled. What sin could he have committed before he was born that would deserve this punishment? And if it was his parents who sinned, why should their son have to suffer?

Jesus sometimes did describe suffering as the result of sin. (For example, when he healed the man who couldn't walk, he told him, "Stop sinning or something worse may happen to you.") But Jesus' general understanding of suffering seems to have been much broader: It could have a variety of known and unknown causes.

In this case, instead of discussing the *cause* of the suffering, Jesus recognizes its potential *purpose*: It's an opportunity for the "works of God" to be displayed. Jesus, always sensitive to the Father's heart, realizes that in this situation a man's suffering can be relieved, that the man can be invited to faith, and Jesus' own identity can be further revealed.

⮑ When we suffer, or a loved one suffers, we often want to know why this is happening. But we have a suggestion here that there may not be a clear answer to this question of the cause, and we should look instead for the potential purpose of the suffering. Have you had an experience where you've been able to see purpose in suffering, even if you never understood its cause? Talk about that experience and what you learned from it.

2 John has been revealing Jesus as the "light of the world" throughout this gospel. As early as the prologue he tells us, "The true light that gives light to everyone was coming into the world." But in this episode the theme of light is explored in more complex ways. Light is connected with sight and faith, knowledge and goodness, and the opportunity to do God's work.

Sight and faith: A connection is established between being in the light and "coming and seeing" who Jesus is (as his first disciples did). The blind man whose sight was restored asks, "Who is [the Son of Man]?" Jesus replies, "You have now seen him."

Knowledge and goodness: To be in the light is also to recognize and acknowledge the truth. But a person can be in the light, see the truth, and refuse it, as the Pharisees do here. Rejecting the light brings spiritual guilt. But being in darkness in the sense of ignorance (lacking knowledge) doesn't bring guilt. (This is different from *hiding* in the darkness to cover up evil deeds, as was described earlier in the gospel.) Jesus tells the Pharisees, "If you were blind, you would not be guilty of sin; but now that you claim you can see, your guilt remains."

Doing God's work: Daylight is the time when God's work can still be done. When night comes, the time for that work is over. Thus light and darkness also describe the time of Jesus' mission and the time when it must end in his death.

⊃ In which of these ways do you most want to move more into the light right now?

   a. Having a better understanding of who Jesus is.

   b. Being freer from the kind of things that people try to hide.

   c. Recognizing better where God is at work, and knowing better how to join in that work.

   d. Some other way.

3 In the last part of the discourse, Jesus changes techniques in a further attempt to be understood. He talks about believing as *hearing* rather than *seeing*. And instead of continuing to interpret the sign he has just performed, he talks about himself using the figure of a flock of sheep and its shepherd.

(This was a common image in the Old Testament for the people of God and their leaders. To give just one example, Psalm 77 ends, "You led your people like a flock by the hand of Moses and Aaron.")

Jesus develops various parts of the image, but his main point remains constant: His true "sheep" will hear and recognize his voice, and follow him. (Significantly, even before the man who was born blind could *see*, he *heard* Jesus' voice and obeyed him, and this led him to believe.)

⤺ Jesus says that he calls his sheep by name, and they follow him because they recognize his voice. They won't follow strangers, because they don't recognize their voices. Who or what is "calling your name" besides Jesus right now? By what name are they calling you? Is Jesus calling you by a new name?

⤺ Take a few moments in silence to listen for the voice of the Good Shepherd. Share with the group anything you hear.

JESUS GOES TO JERUSALEM FOR HANUKKAH

Gospel of John > Book of Signs >
Sixth Section: Jesus and the Festival of Dedication

INTRODUCTION

This section of the Book of Signs describes a journey that Jesus takes to **Jerusalem** for Hanukkah (known as the Festival of Dedication in the gospel of John). This festival commemorates the rededication of the temple and its altar around 165 BC. The Jews recaptured the temple after an enemy empire invaded and desecrated it. Jesus continues to reveal his identity against the backdrop of this festival.

At the end of the section, Jesus leaves Jerusalem, but he doesn't go back to **Galilee**. Instead, he goes across the Jordan to where John was baptizing at first (probably to **Bethany,** although perhaps to **Aenon/Salim**.) This places him only a short journey away from Jerusalem, where he will soon return for a last Passover. Like the other sections of the Book of Signs, this one concludes with a report that many people *believed* in Jesus.

READING

Have several members of your group each read a paragraph of this section. It begins, "Then came the Festival of Dedication . . ." and ends, "And in that place many believed in Jesus."

DISCUSSION

1 The Jewish leaders have had several months to consider what Jesus meant when he called himself the "good shepherd" at the Festival of Tabernacles. They now wonder if he was claiming to be a royal shepherd like David—a Messianic king. They surround him and insist on an answer. But instead of "telling them plainly," as they demand, he once again uses his figure of the shepherd and sheep.

➲ Why does Jesus appeal to stories and figures in situations like this, instead of "speaking plainly"? (There's a suggested answer at the end of this study. If you want, you can read this suggestion and discuss it.)

2 As Jesus explains his identity to his challengers, he asserts, "I and the Father are one." They consider this blasphemy: "You, a mere man, claim to be God." To defend himself, Jesus appeals to the Scriptures. He notes that Psalm 82 refers to people who are judges and receive the word of God. (That is, they're granted God's perspective so they can settle disputes fairly.) The psalm figuratively calls these people "gods." Jesus argues that if people *that the word of God came to* can be called "gods" in this sense, certainly he can be called God in a truer sense, since he is *the Word of God that has come.* (There's an echo of the prologue here: "The Word became flesh" and "coming into the world.") Thus, Jesus argues, the Scriptures themselves give him the right to speak this way. And, he observes again, his works confirm that he is who he claims to be.

➲ How can Jesus, who really is a human being, also be God?

3 Jesus describes himself as the one "whom the Father *set apart.*" This term literally means "consecrated" or "made holy," that is, dedicated for a special purpose. The occasion of this festival is the rededication of the temple and its altar. So Jesus is claiming once again that the places and celebrations that express the heritage of God's people find their ultimate expression in him. He is the true temple, the dwelling place of God ("the Father is in me"). He is the true altar, where the relationship is restored between God and people ("I give them eternal life"). But Jesus has also been "set apart" and "sent into the world" to fulfill a specific mission. As he said when he first used the shepherd figure, "the good shepherd lays down his life for the sheep" and will die as the Savior of the world.

⟳ In his prayer later in the gospel of John (in the Book of Glory), Jesus will ask God to "sanctify" (set apart) his own followers. He will say that he has "sent them into the world" just as the Father has sent him into the world. What things about a person point to the special mission and life purpose that God has set them apart for? (For example, their personality, abilities, place of birth. What else?)

⟳ Can you describe some aspects of your own life mission? If you can't think of any right away, ask the others in your group what they've observed.

NOTES

Suggested answer to question 1: Jesus can't deny that he is the Messiah, but he can't claim to be the kind of Messiah the Jewish leaders are thinking of. So either a "yes" or a "no" answer would be misleading. By returning to his figure of speech, Jesus can explain why the leaders don't already know the answer to their question, and why they're framing it in a way that has no right answer. The works Jesus has already done reveal clearly who he is. But because these leaders are "not his sheep," they don't believe what the works are telling them.

JESUS RAISES LAZARUS FROM THE DEAD

**Gospel of John > Book of Signs >
Seventh Section: Jesus and the Resurrection > Jesus in
Bethany**

INTRODUCTION

The seventh and final section of the Book of Signs describes a journey that Jesus takes back into Judea from across the Jordan. He goes to **Bethany**, a village near Jerusalem, to help his friends Mary and Martha when their brother Lazarus dies. When Jesus raises Lazarus from the dead, this creates so much notoriety that he withdraws briefly to the edge of the Judean desert. But he then goes to **Jerusalem** for the Passover festival. We'll look at the trip into Jerusalem in session 13. In this session, we'll consider the first part of this section, where Jesus raises Lazarus from the dead in Bethany.

READING

Read aloud the accounts of Jesus raising Lazarus from the dead and the meeting of the Sanhedrin afterwards. (The Sanhedrin members were the Jews' religious and political leaders.) Assign parts to different speakers and read these episodes like a play. You'll need people to take these parts:

Jesus raises Lazarus from the dead. (This episode begins, "Now a man named Lazarus was sick.")

> Narrator
> Jesus
> his disciples
> Thomas
> Martha
> Mary
> Jewish guests

 The Sanhedrin meets. (It begins, "Therefore many of the Jews who had come to visit Mary . . ." and ends, "But the chief priests and the Pharisees had given orders that anyone who found out where Jesus was should report it so that they might arrest him.")

> Sanhedrin members
> Caiaphas
> Passover visitors

DISCUSSION

1 As the Book of Signs progresses, more and more profound aspects of Jesus' identity are disclosed. The next-to-last sign, the healing of the man who was born blind, reveals that Jesus is the *light* of the world. This last sign, the resurrection of Lazarus, shows that he is the resurrection and the *life*. (As the prologue says, "In him was *life*, and that life was the *light* of all people." Or, as the guests ask, "Could not he who opened the *eyes* of the blind man have kept this man from *dying*?" The answer is yes, and it's not too late even now, because Jesus is both the light and the life.)

Raising Lazarus from the dead is such a dramatic display of Jesus' power and authority that the Sanhedrin members are very concerned. They're afraid the Romans will think Jesus is going to lead an insurrection, and that Rome will invade Jerusalem to prevent this. (Political power interprets every threat politically. "It's either us or him," Caiaphas argues.)

But the point of this sign is not primarily that Jesus has the ability to do these powerful things. It's that he's the one who gives resurrection life.

Martha is expecting a resurrection "at the last day." Jesus doesn't discourage this expectation, but he insists that the resurrection can also be a present reality for everyone who believes in him. Yes, it provides hope for resurrection after death ("anyone who believes in me will live, even though they die"). But it also imparts a spiritual life now that will never end in spiritual death ("whoever lives by believing in me will never die").

➲ Have you experienced a personal "resurrection" through faith in Jesus? What was your life like before this happened? How is it different now? If you don't think you have experienced a "resurrection" like this, how do you think it could happen for you?

2 The physical resurrection of Lazarus was an exceptional sign that revealed an essential aspect of Jesus' identity as the time of his own death and resurrection approached. But ordinarily, believers in Jesus have to grieve and ultimately accept the physical death of their loved ones. (In this episode, Jesus himself says there is a kind of sickness that "leads to death." He also participates in, and affirms, earthly grief by being deeply moved and troubled, even weeping, though he will soon raise Lazarus from the dead.)

➲ When you have lost loved ones, how has God met you in your grief? Have you been able to challenge and question God, as both sisters seem to do? (They each say to Jesus, "If you had been here, my brother would not have died.") Have you had the assurance that God was present and in deep sympathy with you, as Jesus was with these sisters?

➲ What encouragement would you offer from your own faith experience to someone who might lose a loved one?

3 Jesus doesn't go to Bethany when he first learns that Lazarus is sick. Instead, he waits two days, and only arrives after Lazarus has died. While Martha and Mary, and their guests, seem to believe that the best thing Jesus could have done was to keep Lazarus from dying, Jesus says to his disciples, "for your sake I am glad I was not there" (while he was still alive). The resurrection of Lazarus demonstrates God's power and reveals Jesus' identity in a way that even a miracle of healing might not have.

⮑ Have you ever had an experience where you were hoping and praying that God would do something, but it didn't happen right then? Maybe later on something even better happened (as in this episode), or maybe nothing like an answer to your prayer has happened yet. If you feel comfortable talking about your experience, share what you were hoping and praying for, and why you think things have turned out the way they have so far.

JESUS GOES TO JERUSALEM FOR PASSOVER

**Gospel of John > Book of Signs >
Seventh Section: Jesus and the Resurrection > Jesus in
Jerusalem**

INTRODUCTION

The rest of this section of the Book of Signs relates three episodes that take place when Jesus goes to Jerusalem for a final Passover festival:

- Mary anoints Jesus at a dinner in her home.
- Jesus enters Jerusalem to the acclaim of the crowds.
- Some Greeks ask Philip to introduce them to Jesus.

The Book of Signs then concludes with a summary review of its central themes. It reflects on how people either have or haven't *believed* in Jesus, now that he has "performed so many signs in their presence." The Book of Signs ends with Jesus in the city of Jerusalem just before Passover begins. The Book of Glory will go on to describe what Jesus says and does at that festival.

READING

Have four different members of your group each read one of the remaining parts of this section:

Mary anoints Jesus at a dinner in her home. (This episode begins, "Six days before the Passover . . .")

Jesus enters Jerusalem to the acclaim of the crowds. ("Meanwhile a large crowd of Jews found out that Jesus was there . . .")

Some Greeks ask Philip to introduce them to Jesus. ("Now there were some Greeks . . .")

Conclusion and summary of themes. (It begins, "Even after Jesus had performed so many signs . . ." and ends, "So whatever I say is just what the Father has told me to say.")

DISCUSSION

1 The Book of Signs ends as it began, with a symbolic week. John says it is now "six days before the Passover." Jesus' glory was revealed on the seventh day of the opening week, when he did his first miracle at Cana. It will be revealed supremely at the end of this concluding week, through his death, resurrection, and return to the Father. These events will be related in the Book of Glory.

But here at the start of the week, Mary's actions anticipate those events. She anoints Jesus to honor him and express her thanks. When she's criticized for the extravagance of this gesture, Jesus defends her by interpreting it as preparation for his burial, an anticipation of his sacrificial death.

⮑ Which of these potential responses to the criticism of Mary do you find convincing? If you don't find them convincing, how would you correct them?

a. It's all right to spend extravagantly on the most important life events, like weddings and funerals, to honor our loved ones. Hey, didn't Jesus make hundreds of gallons of wine for the wedding at Cana?

b. When someone asks you for money for a charitable cause, you've got to be really careful. Sometimes it's a scam. Mary knew enough not put any money in the hands of Judas. It's better to spend your money on something that means a lot to you than to give it to a con artist.

c. This was a once-in-a-lifetime opportunity for Mary to show her devotion to Jesus publicly and personally. If you get a chance like that, you've got to commit some resources to it.

⮑ What do you think Jesus meant when he said, "You will always have the poor among you?" (There's a suggested answer at the end of this study that you can interact with.)

2 The Passover crowds, chafing under Roman occupation, express nationalistic sentiments as they welcome Jesus. They call him the "king of Israel" and wave palm branches, a symbol of power and authority. They're hoping Jesus will bring them military and political liberation. But Jesus responds by dramatizing his humble and peaceful character. He enters Jerusalem "lowly and riding on a donkey." This fulfills a prophecy in the book of Zechariah (in the first poetic oracle in that book).

⮑ Does Jesus' symbolic action here rule out the use of coercive power (such as military force) by his followers in the world? Are followers of Jesus limited to non-violent means such as protests, boycotts, and civil disobedience? If not, under what circumstances could force be used to resist powers and institutions that are in active opposition to Jesus' purposes for the world?

3 The prophecy in Zechariah goes on to say that Jerusalem's king will "proclaim peace to the nations" and rule "to the ends of the earth." The eternal life (both present and future) that Jesus will offer to all people is illustrated when some Greeks (Gentiles) now ask to meet him.

The theme that Jesus will gather followers from beyond the borders of Israel has already been struck at several places in the gospel of John. For example, Jesus, as the "good shepherd," says that he has "other sheep that are not of this sheep pen. . . . They too will listen to my voice, and there shall be one flock and one shepherd." When Caiaphas says that one man must die for the Jewish nation, John comments that Jesus will die "not only for that nation but also for the scattered children of God, to bring them together and make them one."

(This same theme may be struck in the ironic question the Jews ask about whether Jesus will "go where our people live scattered among the Greeks, and teach the Greeks." He doesn't do that personally, but by the time this book was written, his followers had.)

When Jesus learns that news of his ministry has reached the Gentiles, and that some are interested in meeting him, he announces, "The hour has come for the Son of Man to be glorified."

⊃ Why would a breakout beyond the nation of Israel signal the end of Jesus' earthly ministry and the time for him to "lifted up from the earth" and die on the cross? (Once again there's a suggested answer at the end of this study that you can interact with.)

4 At the end of the Book of Signs, people's believing and unbelieving responses to Jesus are recorded. In some cases, we're told, people don't believe because they've been spiritually blinded. (The context of the quotation from Isaiah shows that this happens as a judgment on those who have already been stubbornly resisting God.)

In other cases, people believe but are afraid to acknowledge Jesus, because they fear the authorities. This is a warning to readers in John's own day. They too are in danger of being "put out of the synagogue" if they follow Jesus. But they shouldn't "love human glory more than the glory of God," so they must be prepared to suffer disgrace for their faith if necessary.

After these responses of belief and unbelief are recorded, Jesus speaks again. Since no setting is provided for his words, we may understand this as a review of some of the notable things that have been said by or about Jesus to this point. (For example, the statement here, "I did not come to judge the world, but to save the world," echoes what John writes after the conversation with Nicodemus: "God did not send his Son into the world to condemn the world, but to save the world through him.") The gospel of John begins with a prologue that introduces its themes and motifs, and the Book of Signs ends with a review of these themes.

◐ Which of Jesus' statements in this conclusion to the Book of Signs do you find most meaningful at this point in your study of the gospel of John?

NOTES

Suggested answer to question 1: When Jesus says, "You will always have the poor among you," he doesn't mean we should accept chronic, institutionalized poverty. We should do relief and development work, and fight injustice. Jesus wants us to end poverty and oppression. By "the poor" here, he means widows and orphans. Even in a world without injustice, people would sometimes still be impoverished through accidents and misfortune. Caring for these people should be part of our ongoing work. Outside of this ordinary work, there will sometimes be extraordinary opportunities to express lavish devotion to God, as Mary does here.

Suggested answer to question 3: The prologue says, "His own did not receive him. Yet to all who did receive him, to those who believed in his name, he gave the right to become children of God." It may be that the spiritual openness that's now being granted to the Gentiles, who include many of the "scattered children of God," is a signal to Jesus that "his own did not receive him," and there's nothing more he can do to change their response. This would be another illustration of how Jesus is sensitive to every indication he gets of the work the Father is doing.

FOR YOUR NEXT MEETING

If you did session 14 when you did session 2 and read the whole gospel in one sitting, go right to session 15 for your next meeting.

READING THE BOOK OF GLORY

INTRODUCTION

You are now coming to the second main part of the gospel of John, the Book of Glory. It has three sections.

The first and longest section describes the meal that Jesus shared with his disciples on the last night of his life. This section relates the encouragement and instructions Jesus gave them that night as he said goodbye to them and prepared them for his departure. (The discourses in the Book of Signs typically interpret events *after* they happen; in this last discourse Jesus explains the meaning of the most significant event of all, his death, *before* it happens.)

The second section of the Book of Glory describes how Jesus was arrested and interrogated, put on trial, and executed by crucifixion. (Jesus spoke of his death as the "hour of his glory.")

The third section tells how Jesus rose from the dead and appeared to his disciples.

An epilogue to the gospel of John describes one more resurrection appearance.

Note: In the Book of Glory we meet a character for the first time who's described as "the disciple whom Jesus loved" or "another disciple." This seems to be John's way of referring to himself within his own gospel. It may reflect his desire to keep the focus on Jesus, not the author, and it may also show that John has come to understand Jesus' love for him as the most important thing about himself.

READING

Have group members take turns as you read the rest of the gospel of John. The Book of Glory begins with Jesus sharing a meal with his disciples on the night before Passover. In *The Books of The Bible,* this is right after the major break on page 1760. If you have another Bible version, begin reading where you left off at the end of session 13.

This reading should take about forty minutes. Change readers every time you come to the end of what seems like an episode or a major piece of discourse. If you have *The Books of The Bible,* change readers when you come to one of the breaks indicated by white space in the text.

As you hear this part of the book read, you can follow the outline on page 8. Listen for how the major themes introduced in the prologue and developed in the Book of Signs are continuing to unfold.

DISCUSSION

➲ What things struck you most as you heard the Book of Glory being read? What are your overall impressions from this part of the gospel of John?

➲ Which of the things that Jesus said to his disciples at the meal did you find most meaningful?

➲ Which episode after the meal would you most like to have witnessed in person? What would your vantage point have been?

➲ Which character in the whole gospel of John, besides Jesus, do you most identify with? Why?

JESUS WASHES HIS DISCIPLES' FEET

INTRODUCTION

The first section of the Book of Glory describes how Jesus shared a meal with his disciples when they were all in Jerusalem together for the Passover festival, on the night before he gave his life as the Savior of the world. Because this section is so long and important, we'll devote the next seven sessions to it:

Session 15: Before the meal, Jesus washes his disciples' feet.

Sessions 16 through 20: After the meal, Jesus speaks at length with his disciples to prepare them for his departure.

Session 21: Jesus prays for his disciples, and for others who will *believe* in him through their testimony.

In this session, we'll begin by looking at the footwashing.

READING

The footwashing story has three episodes. Have three teams from within your group read one of these episodes out loud like a play, taking the parts that are listed.

 Jesus washes the disciples' feet. (This episode begins, "It was just before the Passover Festival. Jesus knew that the hour had come for him to leave this world . . .")

> Narrator
> Jesus
> Peter

 Jesus explains what he's done. ("When he had finished washing their feet . . .")

> Narrator
> Jesus

 Jesus predicts he will be betrayed. (It begins, "After he had said this, Jesus was troubled in spirit . . ." and ends, "And it was night.")

> Narrator
> Jesus
> Peter
> John ("the disciple whom Jesus loved")

DISCUSSION

1 In the time of Jesus, people walked on dusty roads wearing sandals. It was a courteous gesture of hospitality to provide guests with water to wash their own feet when they arrived in a home. In more affluent homes, a servant might be assigned to wash guests' feet. But by performing this task himself, Jesus is offering humble and loving service to his followers. He explains that he's providing a model he wants them to follow in their relationships with one another: "I have set you an example that you should do as I have done for you." Jesus wants relationships in the community of his followers to be based on a commitment and desire to serve others.

➲ Who do you know who best models this kind of humble service, following Jesus' example? What kinds of things do they do for other people?

2 Beyond setting an example of humble service, Jesus also seems to have been predicting his death through the footwashing, and inviting his disciples to accept his death as an act on their behalf. John says literally that Jesus "lay down" his outer garments to wash his disciples' feet, and that he then "took up" his garments again afterwards. The language is intentionally reminiscent of what Jesus said about himself as the good shepherd who "lays down" his life for his sheep: "I *lay down* my life—only to *take it up* again. No one takes it from me, but I *lay it down* of my own accord. I have authority to *lay it down* and authority to *take it up* again." The outer garments symbolize Jesus' human life, which he gave up for others, and which was then restored to him.

Jesus says to Peter, "Unless I wash you, you have no part with me." This doesn't mean that the footwashing itself conveys salvation. But Peter does have to be willing to accept this act of self-giving on the part of Jesus. If he can receive it now, in principle, he will be open to what Jesus will soon do for him on the cross. "You do not realize now what I am doing," Jesus tells him, "but later you will understand."

➲ Why would a person be unwilling to accept another person's offer of humble, sacrificial self-giving? Complete this sentence to describe the hesitations they might be feeling: "I'm sorry, I can't let you do this, because . . ."

➲ How could a person overcome their hesitations and accept sacrificial gifts from others, especially from Jesus?

3 One of the guests at the meal, Judas Iscariot, has already decided to refuse what Jesus is offering. He has given in to the temptations of the devil and rejected the ideals that Jesus is teaching and modeling. Jesus is so troubled by this rejection that he speaks openly of it. When two of his disciples ask him who he's talking about, he gives a sign that both identifies Judas and demonstrates the hardened state of Judas's heart.

For a host to offer a guest a choice morsel of food was a special gesture of honor and welcome, and an intimate expression of hospitality. Since Judas was opposed to Jesus' mission, he shouldn't have accepted this gesture. He should have shown honesty and integrity by expressing his differences and not sharing friendship rituals unless these differences could be resolved. But Judas deceptively accepted the expression of honor and friendship, showing that he'd chosen a course of treachery.

John observes aptly at the end of this account, "It was night." Jesus had warned, right at the end of the Book of Signs, "You are going to have the light just a little while longer. Walk while you have the light, before darkness overtakes you." The darkness has overtaken Judas, and the night, "when no one can work," has arrived.

⮑ What aspects of Jesus' example and teaching do you think Judas rejected? How would Judas have tried to describe the values and ideals that he held, in contrast to the ones he thought Jesus was proclaiming?

⮑ How would Judas have justified deception and betrayal within the value system he was adopting? (Warning: Be careful as you put yourself inside Judas's head and try to articulate how he would have justified deception and betrayal. It's always hazardous to engage in rationalization that's contrary to Jesus' teachings, even in a teaching-learning exercise. When C.S. Lewis wrote *The Screwtape Letters*, he said it had been dangerous to his own character to try to think like a devil. Use extreme caution.)

JESUS SPEAKS WITH HIS DISCIPLES ABOUT HIS DEPARTURE

Gospel of John > Book of Glory >
First Section > Discourse >
Jesus is the Way, the Truth, and the Life

INTRODUCTION

After recording how Jesus washed the disciples' feet, the first section of the Book of Glory relates a long discourse between Jesus and his disciples. Like the discourses in the Book of Signs, this one develops as Jesus explains and clarifies statements in response to confusion and misunderstanding. But there are a couple of important differences from the earlier discourses.

For one thing, those discourses interpreted signs *after* they were performed, while this last one interprets Jesus' "departure" (his death and resurrection) *before* it happens. And while the earlier discourses tended to develop a single theme (such as "I am the light of the world"), in this long discourse a number of themes are woven together. Like the motifs in a symphony, they appear, fade out, and then recur in a complex pattern of interaction.

The themes in this last discourse include:

Jesus' departure and return
the imperative of love
encouragement to ask in Jesus' name
keeping Jesus' commandments

the coming of the Holy Spirit (the "Advocate")

"remaining" in Jesus

the hostility of the world

Because these themes are woven together so intricately, it's difficult to divide this discourse into discrete sections. But the discourse is so rich and dense that it should nevertheless be considered closely and carefully, not all at once in a single study. Therefore, we'll devote five studies to it. We'll start in this study with the material that *precedes* the first mention of the Holy Spirit.

READING

Have the members of your group take turns reading aloud, one paragraph at a time. Start at the beginning of the discourse ("When he was gone, Jesus said, 'Now is the Son of Man glorified . . .'"). Stop reading just before the first mention of the Holy Spirit. (End with "You may ask me for anything in my name, and I will do it.")

DISCUSSION

1 While this discourse introduces a number of themes right away (such as "love one another"), it begins by focusing primarily on Jesus' departure, since this provides the occasion for all of the other instructions. Jesus announces that he's going to a place where the disciples cannot come. Peter asks where he's going. But it seems he actually wants to know why he can't come along, since Jesus replies, "Where I am going, you cannot follow now."

Peter may suspect that Jesus is talking about his own death, because he replies, "Why can't I follow you now? I will lay down my life for you." Jesus explains that Peter really can't follow him now. Peter isn't as ready as he thinks to "lay down" his life, as Jesus is going to do. Peter will actually deny Jesus this very night, to save his own life. However, when Peter's faith and devotion are stronger, he will indeed "follow later." Peter did give his life for Jesus many years after this, when he died as a martyr under the Roman emperor Nero.

⮑ Is there a way you'd like to follow Jesus' example and teaching, but you don't feel ready to yet? What practical steps can you take to reach the point where you are ready?

⮑ Do you believe you'd literally give up your life for Jesus? Explain.

2 Jesus encourages his disciples not to be troubled, even though he's leaving. He tells them, first of all, that he'll come back and bring them to be with him. (This may refer to his return at the end of history. But it seems to indicate more immediately his return from the dead through the resurrection. This will open the way for people to join him in an intimate, abiding relationship with the Father.)

Jesus also encourages his disciples by telling them that even though they don't know where he's going, they do know the way there. When asked about this, he explains, "I am the way and the truth and the life. No one comes to the Father except through me."

⮑ How would you respond to someone who says it's intolerant of other religious and cultural traditions to present Jesus as the only way to God? (There's a suggested answer at the end of this session that you can interact with after doing your own reflection.)

3 Jesus' statement about being "the way" answers the question about where he's going. He's returning to the Father. But it also gives the disciples the assurance that they can still remain closely connected to Jesus, by entering into the intimacy that he already shares with the Father. Jesus says that if we enter into this kind of relationship with him and his Father, "I will do whatever you ask in my name, so that the Father may be glorified in the Son."

This is not an unconditional promise that Jesus will do "whatever we want." And the condition isn't that we have to use certain words ("in Jesus' name"). The condition is that our request has to be the kind of thing Jesus himself would ask, out of his sensitivity to the work that the Father wants to do in any given situation. (This, as we saw in the Book of Signs, was how the

Father was glorified in Jesus.) Thus "whatever" means "whatever you need to fulfill the Father's purposes," not "whatever you desire for yourself."

⮑ Can you give an example of something that you, or someone you know, has asked for in great confidence, knowing that it expressed the heart of God in a situation and that it would bring glory to God? How was this prayer answered?

NOTES

Suggested answer to question 2: The gospel of John definitely presents Jesus as God's unique provision for the salvation of humanity. Jesus is the pre-existent Word of God who took on human form. This isn't true of any other religious teacher or leader. However, John speaks of Jesus drawing people in from many different backgrounds, rather than excluding anyone based on their background. Jesus is the "Lamb of God, who takes away the sin of the world." His death was "not only for [the Jewish] nation but also for the scattered children of God, to bring them together and make them one." In other words, John envisions genuine "children of God" scattered among the many nations of the earth, and Jesus gathering them together. This vision is inclusive rather than exclusive. When many of these "scattered children" from outside the nation of Israel became followers of Jesus in the first century, it was determined that they didn't need to adopt the customs and practices of Judaism. It may be that many Christian cultural and religious practices today don't need to be duplicated by people from other backgrounds who come to believe in Jesus themselves. In fact, some of their own practices may be preserved and retained as means of expressing their devotion to him.

JESUS PROMISES HIS DISCIPLES THE HOLY SPIRIT

Gospel of John > Book of Glory > First Section > Discourse > Promise of the Spirit

INTRODUCTION

As the last discourse continues, it now introduces the Holy Spirit. It develops the theme of expressing love for Jesus by keeping his commandments. And it describes the unity of life that believers can have with Jesus and the Father.

READING

Have one member of your group read the next section of this discourse aloud, starting with, "If you love me, keep my commands. And I will ask the Father . . ." and ending with, "Come now; let us leave."

DISCUSSION

1 Just before this part of the discourse, Jesus tells his followers they can ask for anything in his name, so that the Father will be glorified. Now he describes something that he's going to ask from the Father: "another advocate" to be with his followers in his absence. The term translated "advocate" here means literally "someone you call to your side." It can describe a legal representative (an "advocate" in the sense of a lawyer). But it can also refer to someone who helps in a more personal capacity, and so it can also be translated "comforter" or "counselor."

Jesus has been a companion, guide, and friend to the disciples while he's been on earth. Now that he's departing, he'll ask the Father to send them "another" advocate to fill this role: the Holy Spirit, who will remain with them and live in them while Jesus is gone. Jesus describes the Holy Spirit as the "Spirit of truth" and also explains, "the Advocate . . . will teach you all things and will remind you of everything I have said to you."

⊃ Truth is a key term in the gospel of John. It's associated with a person "coming into the light." (For example, "All those who do evil hate the light, and will not come into the light for fear that their deeds will be exposed. But those who live by the truth come into the light.") As the "Spirit of truth," the Holy Spirit works to draw people into the light so that they can face themselves honestly and begin to live in a way that doesn't need to be concealed. How have you experienced the work of the "Spirit of truth" in your own heart?

⊃ When, if ever, has the Holy Spirit provided you comfort or counsel?

⊃ Another role of the Holy Spirit is to bring the word of God to our minds and give us a greater understanding of it. Can you remember a time when the Spirit has done this for you?

2 In this brief passage, Jesus stresses several times that we express our love for him by carrying out his wishes:

"If you love me, keep my commands."
"Whoever has my commands and keeps them is the one who loves me."
"Anyone who loves me will obey my teaching."

He provides a personal example of this himself: "I love the Father and do exactly what my Father has commanded me."

A legalistic compliance with regulations doesn't constitute love, or even obedience. Rather, love is an intimate relationship and unity of purpose that will naturally be expressed in actions that reflect a knowledge and an embrace of the loved one's wishes and intentions.

⊃ St. Augustine once said, "Love God, and do what you will." (He explained that if the "root of love" is within a person, nothing but good can spring from this root.) What do you think of this advice?

3 Jesus promises that as we draw closer to him in love and obedience, we will begin to take part in the common life he shares with the Father:

"You will realize that I am in my Father, and you are in me, and I am in you."
"Anyone who loves me will be loved by my Father, and I too will love them."
"My Father will love them, and we will come to them and make our home with them."

The word "home" here is the same one that's translated "room" when Jesus says, "My Father's house has plenty of room." It means literally a place where a person would "remain." It's used in coordination with the many other references in this last discourse to believers "remaining" in Jesus, the Spirit "remaining" with believers, and so on. While there's a future sense in which followers of Jesus will dwell with God, there's also a present sense in which the Father and the Son dwell together in believers now.

⊃ Have you ever had people stay with you (or have you ever stayed with people) who had such a great relationship with one another that you felt drawn into that relationship yourself? What characteristics of the relationship drew you in?

⊃ Is God living inside of you? If you would say yes, do you think of the Father, the Son, or the Spirit living in you?

JESUS TELLS HIS DISCIPLES TO REMAIN IN HIM

**Gospel of John > Book of Glory > First Section >
Discourse > Jesus is the True Vine**

INTRODUCTION

As Jesus continues to speak with his disciples, he now makes the last of the seven "I am" statements in the gospel of John: "I am the true vine." Grapes were cultivated throughout the land of Israel. Like the image of the sheep and their shepherd, grapevines and vineyards provided a figure from the nation's agricultural life that was often used to describe people's relationship with God. Isaiah, for example, said in one of his early prophecies, "The vineyard of the LORD Almighty is the house of Israel, and the people of Judah are the vines he delighted in."

But now Jesus presents himself as "the true vine." Jesus has already explained several times that his followers will come from many nations. And so the biblical vine image now expands to include people outside the "house of Israel." All those who believe in Jesus will be like branches that share the life of this "vine." They will have a close relationship and unity of purpose with Jesus and with one another.

READING

Read the next section of this discourse aloud together as a group (in unison). It's the passage where Jesus describes himself as the true vine. It begins, "I am the true vine . . ." It ends, "whatever you ask in my name the Father will give you. This is my command: Love each other."

DISCUSSION

1 The main point of the image Jesus uses here is that just as a branch can bear no fruit if it doesn't remain attached to the vine, so his followers can bear no fruit if they don't "remain" in him. As we saw in session 17, "remaining" in Jesus means cultivating a close relationship and a unity of purpose with him that will enable us to know his intentions and join him in carrying them out. When we do this, Jesus promises, we will "bear fruit."

In other parts of the New Testament, "fruit" refers to the formation of godly character, and it also refers to the people that we help to follow God through our influence and example. These meanings may be partly in view here. But "fruit" seems to be defined most specifically through two parallel statements:

"If you remain in me and I in you, you will bear much fruit."

"If you remain in me and my words remain in you, ask whatever you wish, and it will be done for you."

In other words, we bear "fruit" when we understand God's purposes for the situations around us and are instrumental in helping those purposes be accomplished. Jesus described the relationship he had with the Father that enabled him to be instrumental in this way as his "glory." Here he says similarly, "This is to my Father's *glory*, that you *bear much frui*t, showing yourselves to be my disciples."

➲ When have you seen this kind of fruit produced in your life? In other words, when have you been able to understand God's purposes for particular situations and helped those purposes be accomplished, seeing the power of God work through you and around you?

2 Jesus says that his Father, as the "gardener," will cut off every branch that doesn't bear fruit, and that he will prune (or "clean") every branch that does bear fruit. In both cases the principle is the same: The resources of the vine are being concentrated on its most productive parts.

Making the total vine fruitful requires cutting off unproductive branches entirely. And pruning a branch means cutting off all the stray shoots and tendrils so that the forming fruit will get all the nutrients from the vine.

Jesus tells his disciples (the "branches"), "You are already clean because of the *word* I have spoken to you." Having the "word" of Jesus remain in us means the same thing as "keeping his commands." Both phrases refer to following the entire way of life that Jesus taught and modeled:

- "coming into the light" and living honestly and transparently;
- being in close relationship with the Father, seeing with his eyes, and feeling with his heart; and
- joining in the Father's purposes in every situation.

If we follow this way of life, Jesus says, we will be "fruitful" people and the Father will direct continuing resources to us.

⮑ How has the gardener worked in your life to trim away stray shoots and tendrils that would drain resources away from the fruit God wants you to bear?

3 Jesus tells his disciples, "I no longer call you servants, because servants do not know their master's business. Instead, I have called you friends, for everything that I learned from my Father I have made known to you." Friendship here represents an active partnership among equally informed participants in a common enterprise.

⮑ What songs or hymns do you know that describe Jesus as a "friend"? (If you're not sure of the words and your group has Internet access, look them up online. If your group can't think of many songs, use a search engine.) How is friendship with Jesus portrayed in these songs?

⮑ Write a song or a poem or a letter to Jesus that expresses a desire for your friendship with him to be an active partnership.

JESUS WARNS HIS DISCIPLES ABOUT THE HOSTILITY OF THE WORLD

Gospel of John > Book of Glory > First Section > Discourse > The World and the Spirit

INTRODUCTION

So far in this discourse there have been a few dark hints about the hostility of "the world" to Jesus and his followers. Now this theme comes to full prominence. Jesus describes how the world's refusal to believe in him will lead it to hate and persecute him and his followers.

But at the same time, a counterbalancing theme is reintroduced. Jesus talks about the Holy Spirit once again. He describes how the "Spirit of truth" will come and show the people of "the world" that they've been wrong in what they've believed about Jesus and how they've responded to him.

READING

Have two members of your group read the next two passages in this discourse:

 The world's hostility. This passage begins, "If the world hates you, keep in mind that it hated me first." It ends, "They hated me without reason." (In *The Books of the Bible,* start at the second break on page 1763.)

The Spirit's witness. This passage begins, "When the Advocate comes, whom I will send to you from the Father . . ." and ends, "That is why I said the Spirit will receive from me what he will make known to you." (In *The Books of the Bible,* start with the third break on page 1763 and read until the break on page 1764. If you're using a different translation it may render these phrases differently, but stop just before Jesus says, "In a little while you will see me no more . . ." That's where you'll begin in session 20.)

DISCUSSION

1 The term *world* has several different meanings in the gospel of John. It can mean the earth where people live (Jesus "came into the world"). It can mean the entire human population of the earth ("God so loved the world that he gave his one and only Son"). Both of these uses are positive. But here the term *world* means something negative. It refers to the system of human interests and beliefs that's hostile to the purposes of God.

This negative meaning comes out clearly in the contrast between two statements in this section of the Book of Glory. Earlier we heard that Jesus "loved his own who were *in* the world" (on the earth); here he tells his disciples, "if you *belonged to* the world" (the hostile system), "it would love you as its own." The disciples are living *in* the world, but they are not *of* the world. By living the life that Jesus has taught and modeled for them, they are actually operating in a totally different spiritual realm from those who are *of* the world, even as they occupy the same physical space with them.

This makes them an irritant, and the people *of* the world want to eliminate them. But despite this hostility and opposition, Jesus' followers need to have a continuing presence *in* the world so they can "testify" about him.

⟳ When we recognize that we're living within a system that's opposed to our commitment to Jesus, we may respond by withdrawing: either "going off the grid" physically, or creating a parallel, Christianized system that we feel we can live in safely. The greater challenge is to represent Jesus effectively in a position of influence within the world system itself. Can you give illustrations of the first kind of response (withdrawal)?

⊃ Do you know someone who's a good example of the second response (representing Jesus effectively in the world)? What kind of hostility has this person encountered, and how have they dealt with it?

⊃ How would you describe yourself at the present time?

   a. Engaged with the planet but not part of the system that's hostile to God.

   b. Not part of the hostile system, but not really engaged with the planet either.

   c. On the planet and kind of caught up in the system, too.

   d. Buying into the values of the system but not really engaged anyway.

⊃ Why are you like this right now?

2 The world hates Jesus' followers because it has rejected Jesus' person and message, even though his words and works provide clear evidence he was sent by God. But despite this willful rejection, Jesus will send the Spirit to show the truth to the people of the world. The Spirit will bring a new understanding of three crucial concepts: "sin and righteousness and judgment."

- *Sin:* The Spirit will show people who've refused to believe in Jesus that they're fundamentally guilty of sin, because when people refuse to believe in Jesus, this shows they're resisting God and his purposes in the world.
- *Righteousness:* The Spirit will show people that Jesus is righteous (accepted by God), even though opponents condemned him to death as a guilty criminal. The Spirit will also assure people that if they trust in Jesus, they'll be righteous (accepted by God) too.

- *Judgment:* Jesus told his opponents that they "judged by mere appearances" and "judged by human standards" because their judgment was taking place *within* the world system. The Spirit will show that true judgment is a judgment *of* the world system: this system will be judged and condemned a place of darkness and falsehood.

⮑ For which of these terms—sin, righteousness, and judgment— is there the greatest difference between the way you would have defined it a year ago (and seen it at work in your own life) and the way you would define and identify it now? What are the differences?

JESUS PROMISES HIS DISCIPLES THEY'LL SEE HIM AGAIN

Gospel of John > Book of Glory > First Section > Discourse > Jesus' Return

INTRODUCTION

As this discourse comes to an end, it focuses, as it did at the start, on Jesus' departure. One more time Jesus makes a statement that meets with confusion and misunderstanding, and the discourse develops as he explains what he meant.

Jesus is encouraging his disciples when he says, "In a little while you will see me no more, and then after a little while you will see me." But this doesn't make sense to them, because a moment earlier Jesus said, "I am going to the Father, where you can see me no longer." So will they be able to see him, or won't they? And just how soon is all of this going to happen?

READING

Read the ending of this discourse. Have four members of your group read it aloud like a play (leaving out cues like "Jesus went on to say"). Begin with, "In a little while you will see me no more . . ." and end with, "But take heart! I have overcome the world."

Have one member take the part of Jesus. Have three other members take the part of "some of his disciples," taking turns reading sentences when this part comes up.

DISCUSSION

1 Throughout his life, Jesus has been representing the Father to the people on earth. His method has often been to compare spiritual realities to earthly ones. Earlier, when speaking with Nicodemus, he used the wind to illustrate what it's like to be born of the Spirit. When speaking with the Pharisees, he drew an analogy to sheep and their shepherd. In this discourse, he's already given the example of the vine and branches.

Now he uses another example: a woman feels anguish when she goes into labor, but then experiences great joy when her child is born. This is a figurative interpretation of his statements to the disciples that "in a little while you will see me no more" (the disciples will feel anguish when Jesus dies) and "after a little while you will see me" (they will experience great joy when they see him again).

⊃ Why is figurative language often successful in communicating spiritual realities when non-figurative language is not?

⊃ Use a story or analogy to illustrate an experience you've had with God lately, or to communicate a spiritual insight you've recently received.

2 After offering the illustration of a woman's joy after giving birth, Jesus promises the disciples that "a time is coming when I will no longer use this kind of language but will tell you plainly about my Father." He says that at that time, he will no longer ask the Father for things on his disciples' behalf (as, for example, he is asking the Father for "another advocate" now). Instead, they will ask the Father directly, in Jesus' name.

Jesus is describing a coming situation when the disciples will recognize the unity between the Father and the Son, so that their knowledge of the Son will become direct knowledge of the Father himself. This is one of the most profound and difficult concepts in the gospel of John. But Jesus is suggesting that the disciples will "see" him again through the unity they will have with him and the Father when, after returning to the Father, Jesus is able to reveal the Father directly.

> ⊃ In the gospel of John, Jesus speaks both of his unity with the Father ("Anyone who has seen me has seen the Father") and of their distinct personalities ("the Father is greater than I"). They are one, but they're distinct. What are the dangers of losing sight of either side of this paradox, and saying either that the Father and Son aren't distinct, or that they aren't one?

3 The disciples seem to be most impressed by the way Jesus knows just what they want to ask. This display of prophetic insight convinces them that he "came from God." (Their response is like Nathaniel's, when Jesus said he saw him under the fig tree, or the Samaritan woman's, who said with amazement, "He told me everything I ever did.") This is the kind of immature, unreliable faith that Jesus has been careful not to encourage. He warns his disciples that, despite the zeal they feel for him now, they will soon all abandon him.

> ⊃ Why doesn't a faith that's based on witnessing supernatural displays of power or knowledge sustain a person when they encounter persecution? What provides the strongest grounding to keep a person faithful to Jesus even when following him becomes very costly and difficult?

4 Even though they're going to waver, Jesus leaves his disciples with two great gifts: peace and joy. Earlier he told them, "Peace I leave with you; my peace I give you. . . . Do not let your hearts be troubled and do not be afraid." He renews the gift of peace here.

When he was talking about the vine and the branches, he urged his disciples to keep his commandments and remain in his love "so that my joy may be in you and that your joy may be complete." He promises them the same fullness of joy here. These are personal gifts from him: "my peace" and "my joy."

➲ Describe a time when you experienced peace or joy, despite troubling or distressing circumstances, and knew this was a gift to you from Jesus.

JESUS PRAYS FOR HIMSELF, HIS DISCIPLES, AND HIS FUTURE FOLLOWERS

Gospel of John > Book of Glory > First Section > Prayer

INTRODUCTION

Jesus ends his time together with his disciples by praying to the Father for himself, for them, and for those who will believe in him through their testimony. (This completes the Book of Glory's first section, which describes what happened at the meal that Jesus shared with his disciples on his final night before his death.)

READING

Have several members of your group each read aloud a paragraph of Jesus' prayer. It begins, "After Jesus said this, he looked toward heaven and prayed." It ends, "in order that the love you have for me may be in them and that I myself may be in them."

DISCUSSION

Jesus' prayer is unusual, compared with many of our prayers. In it he makes only a few requests. Instead, as he is talking to the Father, Jesus makes many affirmations of truth ("All I have is yours, and all you have is mine") and statements of what he has accomplished ("I gave them the words you gave me and they accepted them"). He also states what he currently plans to do ("I . . . will continue to make you known").

Within these affirmations and statements, Jesus expresses what his purposes have been ("I sanctify myself, that they too may be truly sanctified") and what he understands the Father's purposes to have been ("you granted him authority . . . that he might give eternal life"). At one point Jesus even expresses a wish ("I want those you have given me to be with me where I am").

In other words, this is much more of a briefing or project summary than what we usually think of as a prayer. The style of Jesus' prayer illustrates his cooperation with the Father. He affirms their common understanding, explains how he has carried out the mission he was given, describes the shared goals he's been pursuing, and says what he'd like to see happen. It's only within this active pursuit of "the work you gave me to do" that he asks the Father for a few specific things that are necessary for that work to be carried on after he leaves the earth.

⊃ Explore this prayer in more depth by having the members of your group, in teams of two or three, look at different paragraphs in it. Have them identify which sentences are:

- requests
- affirmations of truth
- statements of what Jesus has accomplished or plans to accomplish

Have each team report back to the group and list the sentences they've identified.

⊃ Which sentences that you've just identified also express a purpose? (That is, which ones say why Jesus has said or done something?) Example: "I have given them the glory that you gave me, that they may be one as we are one" is a statement of what Jesus has accomplished that also expresses a purpose.

⮑ Which of the requests, wishes, and purposes that Jesus expresses in this prayer would you most like to see fulfilled in your own life? Choose one or two, and explain what it would mean for them to be fulfilled for you. Here's a list to choose from:

- Glorify your Son, that your Son may glorify you
- That he might give eternal life to all those you have given him
- Protect them by the power of your name
- That they may be one as we are one
- That they may have the full measure of my joy within them
- My prayer is not that you take them out of the world but that you protect them from the evil one
- Sanctify them by the truth
- I pray also for those who will believe in me through their message, that all of them may be one
- So that they may be brought to complete unity
- Then the world will know that you sent me and have loved them even as you have loved me
- I want those you have given me to be with me where I am, and to see my glory
- That the love you have for me may be in them and that I myself may be in them.

⮑ During your group's prayer time, try using the "cooperation" model that Jesus demonstrates here: Before you make a request, explain to God what purposes you've been pursuing based on your understanding of the mission God has given you, and describe some things you've already accomplished to fulfill that mission. Then explain how what you're requesting is necessary for you to complete this mission.

JESUS IS ARRESTED, INTERROGATED, AND DENIED

Gospel of John > Book of Glory > Second Section > Arrest

INTRODUCTION

The second section of the Book of Glory describes how Jesus gave his life as the Savior of the world. It tells how he was arrested and interrogated; put on trial; and executed on a cross. We'll look at the different parts of this section over the next three sessions.

READING

In this session, we'll hear the story of how Jesus was arrested and Peter denied him. John tells this story in four scenes, alternating the focus between Jesus and Peter. Have one person read aloud the first and third scenes (where Jesus is the central character), and have another person read the second and fourth scenes (where Peter is the central character).

 Scene 1 (focus on Jesus) begins, "When he had finished praying . . ."

Scene 2 (focus on Peter) begins, "Simon Peter and another disciple were following Jesus."

 Scene 3 (focus on Jesus) begins, "Meanwhile, the high priest questioned Jesus . . ."

 Scene 4 (focus on Peter) begins, "Meanwhile, Simon Peter was still standing there warming himself."

DISCUSSION

1 The account of Jesus' arrest illustrates the truth of his statement that "I lay down my life . . . No one takes it from me, but I lay it down of my own accord." Even though Jesus knows that Judas intends to betray him, Jesus doesn't hide. He goes to a location that Judas is familiar with. And when the soldiers arrive, Jesus steps forward to identify himself. He insists that all of his followers be allowed to go free. He tells Peter not to try to defend him, because he's willing to "drink the cup the Father has given."

Jesus' power over his own life is evident from the way the soldiers fall back when they hear him say "I AM." Their response shows that Jesus isn't just identifying himself; he's declaring the name the Father has given him (as he said in his prayer).

The spiritual weakness of the armed force that has come against Jesus is shown by the way the soldiers are looking for him at night with "torches" and "lanterns." As we've seen, when John includes specific details like this, they're symbolically significant. Jesus' pursuers are guided by the artificial light *of* the world to a person they know only as "Jesus of Nazareth." Their knowledge and understanding are limited to "mere appearances." But those who have walked in the "true light" that has come *into* the world know him instead by a wide array of spiritual names and titles, as we noted in session 3 and have seen throughout John's gospel. These people recognize that Jesus has been sent by the Father.

⮑ Work together as a group to retell this episode from the perspective of one of the soldiers who accompanies Judas.

(Someone with a laptop can record and edit the story as you develop it. Some members of the group may be able to illustrate your story with drawings or sketches.)

How do you understand the mission you're being sent on? Who is Jesus, and why are you looking for him? How do you explain what happens to all the soldiers when Jesus announces his identity? Why don't his followers put up a better fight? What's going to happen to Jesus now? What do you wonder about when you think back over the events of the night?

2 Annas was not the current high priest, but he had held the office in the past and so was still referred to by that title. Several of his family members were high priests after him. He was a senior member of the priestly establishment who had extensive influence and connections—a "godfather" figure.

Jesus was brought to Annas first so he could question him and set a course for the proceedings against him. Annas seems to have believed that Jesus was at the center of a secret, conspiratorial organization.

Jesus explained that there was nothing more to his teaching or his group of followers than appeared openly. Jesus wondered why Annas didn't call witnesses to document his activities. (After all, the Jewish leaders had earlier challenged him, "Here you are, appearing as your own witness; your testimony is not valid.")

One of the soldiers, considering it insolent for Jesus to challenge the high priest this way, struck him. But Jesus insisted he'd said nothing inappropriate or disrespectful. This interrogation demonstrates the truth of Jesus' assertion during the last discourse: "They hated me without reason."

⊃ Why would Annas believe there had to be more to Jesus' teaching and mission than was evident from his public appearances?

3 John alternates the scenes of Jesus before the high priest and Peter in the courtyard. This dramatizes how, even as Jesus is faithfully speaking the truth about himself, Peter is faithlessly denying his relationship with Jesus. Only a short time earlier, Peter had insisted he would lay down his life for him.

⮕ How would you explain the difference between what Peter thought he would do and what he actually did? Was he wrong in the first place about his own commitment? Or did he fail to anticipate the fear and intimidation he'd feel? Or is there some other explanation?

⮕ How can we prepare and equip ourselves to fulfill our own good intentions, even when we encounter more opposition and intimidation than we expected?

THE TRIAL OF JESUS

Gospel of John > Book of Glory > Second Section > Trial

INTRODUCTION

The Book of Glory now describes how Jesus was put on trial by Pilate, the Roman governor of Judea. The moment of Jesus' sacrifice is drawing close, and as it does, John tells the story with increasing reverence and elegance. He gives the narrative a shape that was considered beautiful and refined in Hebrew literature. John relates the story of Jesus' trial in seven episodes. The outermost (first and last) episodes are paired, as are the ones that lie just inside them in the arrangement, and the ones that lie inside those. (A literary pattern built out of nested elements like this is known as a *chiasm*.) Thus:

A: The Jewish Leaders Demand Execution

   B: Pilate Speaks with Jesus About Kingship

      C: Pilate Declares Jesus Innocent;
      the Jewish Leaders Shout for Barabbas

         D: The Soldiers Beat and Mock Jesus

      C: Pilate Declares Jesus Innocent Two More Times;
      the Jewish Leaders Shout for Crucifixion

   B: Pilate Speaks With Jesus About Authority

A: Pilate Agrees to the Demand for Execution

111

READING

Have four members of your group read the account of Jesus' trial. Assign one letter from A to D to each speaker, and have them read the one or two episodes identified by that letter:

A. Begin with, "Then the Jewish leaders took Jesus . . ."

B. Begin with, "Pilate then went back inside the palace . . ."

C. Begin with, "With this he went out again to the Jews . . ."

D. Begin with, "Then Pilate took Jesus and had him flogged."

C. Begin with, "Once more Pilate came out and said to the Jews . . ."

B. Begin with, "When Pilate heard this, he was even more afraid . . ."

A. Begin with, "From then on, Pilate tried to set Jesus free . . ." End with, "Finally Pilate handed him over to them to be crucified."

DISCUSSION

1 The charge against Jesus is that he has claimed to be the "king of the Jews." In other words, he's accused of setting himself up as the leader of a nationalistic uprising against the Romans. But when Pilate questions him, it quickly becomes evident that Jesus is involved in nothing of the kind. He's been proclaiming a spiritual kingdom that is "not of this world."

Nevertheless, the charge against Jesus provides a theme that's explored from different angles throughout the account of his trial. At the very center of the seven-part arrangement here, John describes how the soldiers flog and beat Jesus. They salute him mockingly as the "king of the Jews." But this is one more place in the gospel of John where people ironically say things about Jesus that are far truer than they can imagine, and which will come true in the future. One day many more Gentiles, like these Roman soldiers do mockingly, will genuinely acknowledge Jesus as their king.

⮑ Jesus doesn't deny being a king, but he explains that his kingdom isn't of this world. (Bear in mind the meanings of "world" discussed in session 19.) What kind of king is Jesus? How does he exert his authority? Who or what does he rule? What songs, hymns, or stories do you know that describe how Jesus is a king?

2 The leaders of Jesus' own people, by contrast, are so eager to have him executed that they not only reject him as their king, they renounce their allegiance to the Messiah they've been expecting from the line of David. They insist, "We have no king but Caesar."

This claim will help them get Jesus executed, but they're insincere. When these leaders are given a choice between Jesus and Barabbas, they turn loose the one who's actually been involved in an uprising against Caesar, and they demand the execution of the one who has openly renounced worldly ambitions.

These Jewish leaders weren't acting, in God's eyes, on behalf of their entire nation. Their decision didn't forfeit the spiritual heritage of Israel. Instead, they're just representative of the religious people in every age who surrender too many (if not all) of their spiritual hopes to political calculations. These leaders have been trying to kill Jesus ever since they decided, "If we let him go on like this, everyone will believe in him, and then the Romans will come and take away both our temple and our nation." Because they're trying to hang on to their own political power, they reject Jesus, even though God has sent him as Israel's promised and long-awaited king.

⮑ Have you seen people who say they're trying to fulfill God's purposes move too far from spiritual means into political measures? How can we become aware of, and stop, a drift into behaving as if Jesus' kingdom was "of this world"?

3 The question about Jesus' kingship also reveals the true character of Pilate's authority. While he claims, "I have power either to free you or to crucify you," Jesus insists that the only power Pilate really has is delegated power, "from above." This is the same expression Jesus used with Nicodemus when he told him, speaking of the kingdom of heaven, "You must be born again" or "from above."

All power on earth is actually granted by the Father. (That's why Jesus could say earlier about his own life, "I have authority to lay it down and authority to take it up again. This command I received from my Father.")

Pilate is only carrying out his delegated responsibilities. He's not the person who has set this unjust campaign against Jesus in motion. Nevertheless, he's declared this prisoner innocent three times, and he should insist on releasing him. The fact that he can't, despite what he wants to do and tries to do, shows that he really is powerless. He's too caught up in the currents of political maneuvering to take the "side of truth."

⮑ How does Pilate lose control of the situation here? What compromises and concessions does he make at various points, and what motivates him to do this? What could Pilate have done differently to assert his authority on behalf of justice?

JESUS GIVES HIS LIFE ON THE CROSS

Gospel of John > Book of Glory > Second Section > Crucifixion

INTRODUCTION

The Book of Glory now describes how Jesus died on the cross as the Savior of the world. John continues to relate the momentous events at the end of Jesus' life with great reverence. He presents another chiasm, an elegant pairing of narrative episodes. To describe the crucifixion, John creates this seven-part arrangement:

A: Jesus is Brought to the Place of Execution

  B: Pilate Refuses the Jewish Leaders' Request to Change the Inscription

    C: The Soldiers at the Cross Cast Lots for Jesus' Clothes

      D: Jesus Entrusts Mary into John's Care

    C: The Soldiers at the Cross Give Jesus Wine to Drink

  B: Pilate Grants the Jewish Leaders' Request to Break the Prisoners' Legs

A: Jesus is Taken from the Place of Execution

READING

Have four members of your group read the account of Jesus' crucifixion and burial. Assign one letter from A to D to each speaker, and have them read the one or two episodes that are identified by that letter:

A. Begin with, "So the soldiers took charge of Jesus."

B. Begin with, "Pilate had a notice prepared and fastened to the cross."

C. Begin with, "When the soldiers crucified Jesus . . ."

D. Begin with, "Near the cross of Jesus stood his mother . . ."

C. Begin with, "Later, knowing that everything had now been finished . . ."

B. Begin with, "Now it was the day of Preparation . . ."

A. Begin with, "Later, Joseph of Arimathea asked Pilate for the body of Jesus." End with, "since the tomb was nearby, they laid Jesus there."

DISCUSSION

The meaning of Jesus' death is so profound that ordinary narrative cannot hope to describe or explain it. In an attempt to convey as much of its meaning as possible, John gives his narrative an artistic shape. He also includes many details that serve as evocative symbols, and he makes frequent allusions to Israel's spiritual heritage as recorded in the Scriptures.

1 As the gospel of John reaches its climax, Jesus' identity is finally explored against the background of the Passover Festival. For that festival, lambs were sacrificed to commemorate how God had delivered the people of Israel from slavery in Egypt. Back then, the Israelites applied the blood of lambs to their doorframes so that God's judgment would "pass over" them. Pilate ordered Jesus' execution at noon on the day before Passover, precisely the time when the lambs for the festival were slain.

One of the regulations for the Passover meal was that none of the lamb's bones should be broken, just as Jesus' bones were not broken on the cross. Hyssop was used to apply the lambs' blood to the doorframes; the soldiers here use a hyssop branch to lift a drink up to Jesus on the cross. By including all of these details, John portrays Jesus as the true Passover lamb, confirming John the Baptist's identification of him as the "Lamb of God who takes away the sin of the world."

⮑ What's your favorite worship song, hymn, or poem that describes Jesus as the "Lamb of God" because of his death on the cross? Share it with the group. (If you're not sure of the words and the group has Internet access, use a search engine to find the words. If music videos of some of songs are available online, watch a few together.)

2 John also interprets the meaning of Jesus' death by referring to other Scriptures. In Psalm 22, David describes how he's suffering because he's deathly ill and at the mercy of his enemies. David tells how the people around him, because they're convinced he won't survive, "divide my clothes among them and cast lots for my garment." He also says, "My mouth is dried up like a potsherd, and my tongue sticks to the roof of my mouth." Jesus, the promised king in the line of David, experiences the same kind of sufferings. His clothes are taken and divided (John refers directly to Psalm 22 when describing this), and he suffers from thirst.

⮑ Besides the loss of his possessions and the experience of thirst, Jesus experienced many other kinds of suffering on the cross. He thus identified with all these kinds of suffering that people experience. List as many of them as you can. (You can compare your answers with the suggestions at the end of this study.)

⮑ Are you presently experiencing suffering? If so, how has Jesus has identified with the kind of suffering you're experiencing?

3 John also alludes to the last prophecy in the book of Zechariah to help interpret the piercing of Jesus' side. (John cited this same prophecy earlier, to help disclose Jesus' identity against the background of the Festival of Tabernacles.)

This prophecy predicts that Israel and its ruling house will be brought to tearful repentance: "I will pour out on the house of David and the inhabitants of Jerusalem a spirit of grace and supplication. They will look on me, the one they have pierced, and they will mourn for him . . ." This seems to be a suggestion that Jesus' death will lead many to believe in him. John testifies personally here about what he saw at the cross, "so that you also may believe."

Zechariah's prophecy also says, "On that day a *fountain* will be opened to the house of David and the inhabitants of Jerusalem, to cleanse them from sin and impurity." The flow of water and blood from Jesus' side is another of the evocative symbols in this account, and John may consider it to be this "fountain." The outpouring may symbolically indicate the gift of the Holy Spirit. As we saw earlier, when Jesus promises "streams of living water" at the Festival of Tabernacles, John comments, "By this he meant the Spirit, whom those who believed in him were later to receive."

⊃ What are the spiritual benefits that flow to you from the cross of Jesus? Have your group list as many as you can.

4 At the center of the seven-part arrangement is the episode where Jesus entrusts his mother, Mary, to John's care. Jesus was a person of compassion who extended mercy and care to others right to the very end of his life.

It's interesting that an account of the crucifixion would not have Jesus' actual death at its center. John may have an additional purpose for including this episode and placing it where he does. He may be putting his central focus not on the *fact* of Jesus' death, but on its *effects*. John may be showing how Jesus' death is for "the scattered children of God, to *bring them together* and *make them one*." Through his death, believers in Jesus become part of a new family, which is their true family.

⊃ Are there some followers of Jesus who are "just like family" to you? What creates the bond between you?

NOTES

Suggested answer to question 2: Jesus suffered extreme physical pain, mocking, embarrassment, injustice, false accusations, betrayal, abandonment, rejection, humiliation, separation from his loved ones through death, and hasty burial. Your group may recognize other sufferings he experienced.

JESUS RISES FROM THE DEAD AND APPEARS TO HIS DISCIPLES

Gospel of John > Book of Glory > Third Section

INTRODUCTION

The third section of the Book of Glory describes how God raised Jesus from the dead after his enemies had executed him and how Jesus then appeared to his followers. This section describes three appearances. They take place "early on the first day of the week," "on the evening of that first day of the week," and "a week later."

READING

Read this section out loud like a play. It begins, "Early on the first day of the week . . ." Include the short conclusion that begins, "Jesus performed many other signs . . ." Have people take these parts:

> Narrator
> the angels
> Mary Magdalene
> Jesus
> the disciples
> Thomas

DISCUSSION

When Peter and John are alerted by Mary Magdalene that the tomb is empty, they race to see what has happened. They find the cloths that Jesus was buried in, but his body isn't there anymore. Certainly something extraordinary has happened. There's no reason why anyone who might have moved or stolen the body would have removed the cloths first.

John tells us that he *saw* this and *believed*. Peter's response isn't recorded, but we are told that even though Mary sees the same thing in the tomb (plus a couple of angels!), she continues to think that someone has removed Jesus' body from the tomb. But when Jesus appears and speaks her name, she does recognize him. According to some manuscripts, he calls her by her Hebrew name, "Miriam." (The good shepherd "calls his own sheep by name," and they "know his voice.")

Mary carries the news of Jesus' resurrection to the disciples. When they see Jesus later that day, they are "overjoyed," particularly when they see his wounded hands and side. This is proof that he's come back to life after being crucified. (This fulfills Jesus' prediction that "I will see you again and you will rejoice.")

The other disciples tell Thomas that Jesus is alive, but he refuses to believe unless he sees the same proof himself. When Jesus appears again a week later, he offers Thomas the chance to examine his wounds. (This suggests that Jesus knows some people understand by *seeing*, some by *hearing*, and some by *touch*.) But apparently Thomas doesn't need to do any examination. He exclaims, "My Lord and my God!"

We see that people respond in different ways to the evidence that Jesus has risen from the dead:

- Some see and believe. (John, the disciples)
- Some see and don't believe, but then believe when they hear. (Mary)
- Some hear and don't believe, but then believe when they see. (Thomas)
- Some hear and do believe, even though they haven't seen.

Those in this last category are the ideal readers of this gospel. John has related many of the signs that Jesus did to show who he was. He assures his readers that he could have related many more. But these are sufficient for those blessed people who will believe by hearing, and have life in Jesus' name.

⮑ Now that you've given detailed consideration to the life, death, and resurrection of Jesus, what do you believe about him? If your beliefs have changed while you've gone through the gospel of John, share with the group how they've changed. What have you seen, what have you heard, and how have these things shaped your beliefs? If you want to express your faith in Jesus for the first time, or to renew your commitment to live for Jesus, ask your group to pray with you as you do this.

JESUS APPEARS TO HIS DISCIPLES BY THE SEA OF GALILEE

INTRODUCTION

After the formal conclusion to the gospel of John, another story is told that serves as an epilogue or afterword. Apparently there was a rumor that Jesus said John wouldn't die before he returned to earth. This story sets the record straight: that's not what Jesus said. This story was apparently added to the gospel because John did die, and his death was making people wonder whether they really could trust Jesus' word. If that's why this material was added, then someone other than John must have written and included it. But it nevertheless continues the characteristic language, symbolism, and theological themes of the gospel.

READING

Have two teams read this epilogue aloud like a play. It has two episodes:

Episode 1: The fishing expedition and the breakfast with Jesus on the shore. (It begins, "Afterward Jesus appeared again to his disciples, by the Sea of Galilee.")

Narrator

Peter

the other disciples

Jesus

John

 Episode 2: Jesus' conversation with Peter. (It begins, "When they had finished eating, Jesus said to Simon Peter . . ." and continues to the end of the book.)

Narrator

Jesus

Peter

DISCUSSION

1 The disciples' extraordinary catch of fish resonates with one of the key theological themes of this gospel. Jesus' life on earth was characterized by cooperation with the Father. He said, "the Son can do nothing by himself; he can do only what he sees his Father doing."

In the last discourse, Jesus explained to his disciples that he wanted them to enter into this same kind of cooperation with the Father. He would no longer represent the Father to them; instead, they would relate to the Father directly, as they entered into the Father and Son's own unity with one another. "Remain in me," he told them, because "apart from me you can do nothing."

On their own, the disciples aren't able to catch any fish. But when they do what Jesus tells them, they catch a huge amount of fish. This is likely a symbolic promise that they will succeed in their mission to testify about Jesus and call others to faith in him—if they will carry out this mission in cooperation with him.

➲ Have you seen God prepare the way and create opportunities for you to share your faith in Jesus with others? In other words, on specific occasions and in the lives of specific people, have you been able to join in what God was "already doing" to help them to believe in Jesus?

2 The second part of the epilogue describes how Jesus restores Peter after his denial and appoints him as the "shepherd" of his followers. Peter denied Jesus three different times. Now, by varying the language of his questions and instructions, Jesus gives him the opportunity to affirm his love and loyalty three different times. (See explanation in the Notes section below.)

Jesus also makes the setting of the restoration a charcoal fire, just like the one where Peter had spoken his denials.

Once Peter has affirmed his love, Jesus takes him back to the time before the denial when he insisted, "I will lay down my life for you." Jesus tells him in figurative language that he actually will be able to die for his faith in Jesus. (Tradition says that Peter was executed by the emperor Nero around AD 65.)

⊃ In a tender and meaningful way, Jesus gives Peter a second chance. Do you know someone who's also been given a second chance like this? Have you been given one yourself?

NOTES

Different words are used in various combinations for "love," "feed/care for," and "lambs/sheep." Interpreters of this passage sometimes look for significance in the way two different words for love are used, but the terms are really interchangeable in the gospel of John. Both terms are used, for example, in the phrase "the disciple whom Jesus loved," and both are used to describe Jesus' love for Lazarus.

Bonus discussion opportunity for people who've read and studied the whole gospel of John and haven't gotten enough yet.

Many of the details in this epilogue seem to have symbolic significance. We're told that the "net was not torn," even though it had so many fish in it. This recalls the soldiers' words about Jesus' seamless garment: "Let's not tear it." (The same term is used in both cases. It gives us our word *schism*.) The net and the garment are probably symbols of the community of Jesus' followers, the "scattered children of God" that Jesus has "made one," the "one flock" that has "one shepherd."

The description of the shared meal enhances the symbolic meaning of this account. We're told that Jesus "took the bread and gave it to them, and did the same with the fish." This is almost an exact duplicate of the earlier description of Jesus feeding the five thousand on the shores of this very same lake. As we saw when we considered that episode, it has strong overtones of the Lord's Supper or Eucharist, the sacred meal that unites Jesus' followers into a single community.

⮑ How should the present-day community of Jesus' followers seek to live out the vision for unity and completeness that's expressed here? Do we need to work for organizational unity (reunification)? If not, what tangible forms should our unity take? How do we know when unity is present and when it's absent?

Many interpreters also believe that the exact number of fish in the net, 153, is a detail that has been preserved because it has some symbolic significance. As we've seen many times before, when specific details are included in this gospel, they tend to have a symbolic meaning.

The gospel of John almost always uses round numbers: The first two disciples go to stay with Jesus at "about four in the afternoon." The stone jars in Cana hold "twenty to thirty gallons." Bethany is "less than two miles from Jerusalem." Even here the boat is "about a hundred yards" from shore. So we would expect to hear that there were "about 150" fish in the net. Because an exact number is reported instead, it likely has a symbolic meaning. So why should the writer specify that there were 153 fish in the net?

Many different explanations have been offered, but in general interpreters see this figure as symbolic of the full number of those who will come to believe in Jesus. One explanation is that 153 is a "triangular number." A triangle made of dots, with 17 dots on each side, will have a total of 153 dots in it. The ancient world was fascinated with numbers like this, so many readers would have known that this number pointed to 17, which may itself be symbolic of 7 + 10. Could this mean believers gathered from both the Jewish and Gentile communities?

Interpretations like this are speculative, but this question illustrates that throughout the gospel of John, there are theological insights waiting just beneath the surface. "Throw in your net and you'll find some." This guide has hopefully pointed to a few of the great fishing spots in this inspired book.

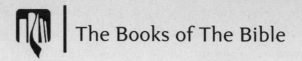

The Books of The Bible

Clean. Beautiful. Unshackled.

- chapter and verse numbers removed
  (chapter and verse range given at bottom of page)
- natural literary breaks
- no additives: notes, cross-references,
  and section headings removed
- single-column setting
- whole books restored (Luke-Acts)
- book order provides greater help in understanding

There is no Bible more suited to reading—from the beginning of the book to the end—than *The Books of The Bible*. This "new" approach is actually the original approach, and I love it.

Scot McKnight
North Park University

For more information or to download the gospel of John, visit http://www.thebooksofthebible.info. Premium editions of this Bible will be available in Spring 2011 from Zondervan at your favorite Christian retailer.

Bible reading is declining at such a rapid rate that within 30 years the Bible will be a "thing of the past" for most Christ-followers. One of the main reasons for this decline is the format of the Bible. The format we know today was created so that a "modern" world could divide and analyze and systematize the Scriptures. But this made the word of God practically unreadable. As we move into a postmodern world, we'll need to recapture the stories, songs, poems, letters, and dreams that naturally fill the pages of Scripture. Only then will a new generation of readers return to the Bible.

Christopher Smith argues in this book that the "time for chapters and verses is over." He explains how these divisions of the biblical text interfere with our reading and keep us from understanding the Scriptures. He describes how Biblica has created a new format for the Bible, without chapters and verses, with the biblical books presented in their natural forms. And he shares the exciting new approaches people are already taking to reading, studying, preaching, and teaching the Bible in this new presentation.

Paperback, 240 pages, 5.5 x 8.5
ISBN: 978-1-60657-044-9
Retail: $15.99

Available for purchase online or through your local bookstore.